D1104509

Humanitarian Woman

MY PERSONAL ENCOUNTERS
WITH
MOTHER TERESA
AND HOW SHE CHANGED
MY LIFE FOREVER

*To Jean
May this book bring you hope,
inspiration and blessings!
Laura Qirko*

LAURA QIRKO
WITH RONDA CHERVIN

Wyatt House Publishing

© Copyright 2020 Laura Qirko

All rights reserved. Permission is granted to copy or reprint portions for any noncommercial use, except they may not be posted online without permission.

Wyatt House books may be ordered through booksellers or by contacting:

Wyatt House Publishing
399 Lakeview Dr. W.
Mobile, Alabama 36695

Because of the dynamic nature of the Internet, any web address or links contained in this book may have changed since publication and may no longer be valid.

Cover design by: Sam Noerr
Interior layout by: Sam Noerr

ISBN 13: 978-1-7345398-8-2

Printed in the United States of America

CONTENTS

CHAPTER 1
A TREASURE FROM ABOVE

On a beautiful Sunday morning in 1991, when I was about five years old, my family and I were visiting my grandparents in Tirana, the capital of Albania.

God gave me the gift of a vivid photographic memory and I remember my childhood as if it were today. When we arrived at my grandparents' house, my mother, Marjeta, greeted her parents and then began to share her dream from the night before.

All the family gathered around my beautiful mother, a young woman with short, curly brown hair. As my mother spoke to us, my father, Frederik, also listened carefully.

In my grandparents' house in Tirana, Albania, 1988.

From left to right: My brother, Dritan, my grandfather Lefter, holding my cousin Artan. My cousin Leand. My grandmother Aleksandra, holding me. My cousin Nensi.

My mother began describing her dream: "I was standing in a huge crowd of people, when suddenly Mother Teresa of Calcutta appeared in her famous white and blue-lined sari. She came right up to me and filled my hands with her special *medalionet e Shenmeris,* medallions of the Madonna [Mary, the mother of Jesus]."

My tiny ears took in every word. It was as if my mother was telling a fairy tale rather than describing a dream. The name Mother Teresa echoed in my mind. Although I was only five years old, too young to fully comprehend the meaning of my mother's dream and the significance of Mother Teresa's appearing in it, the name Mother Teresa would not escape my thoughts.

When I managed to get my mother's attention, I asked, "When can I go out in the sun and play with the other children on the block?"

My mother gave her permission, and full of joy I ran out of the house as fast as I could. While my friends and I were playing, we heard police sirens coming from every direction. Our curiosity grew and we ran to the Cafe Flora Square where a sea of people surrounded us.

As small children often do, we made our way through the crowd to discover what was happening. In the midst of the craziness, we discovered a Red Cross minivan. The center of attention seemed to be a tiny, wrinkled old woman wearing a white sari with blue stripes. Her face was as radiant as an angel. Wearing a warm smile, she was coming out of the van to greet the gathering crowd of people.

At first I was afraid because I had no idea who this woman was. But as soon as my eyes caught her sincere smile filled with love, I felt at ease.

All I could hear around me were the words *"Nënë Teresa! Nënë Teresa!,"* which in Albanian means Mother Teresa. Everything was so strange and I wondered why the people were calling this woman Mother Teresa. I didn't make the connection that this woman was the Mother Teresa of Calcutta who had appeared in my mother's dream.

Surrounded by the huge crowd of people, suddenly Mother Teresa pointed directly at me. Her small wrinkled finger had rosary beads around it. She beckoned to me as she said, *"Hajde!"* In Albanian that means "come."

I was filled with many mixed emotions. I was afraid to approach a stranger but, at the same time, deep inside my heart I was excited to be the first person asked to come to her. It was as if someone was whispering in my ear that it was okay because she was a very special person. As I made my way toward Mother Teresa, her eyes sparkled with joy and her smile was filled with love. She took my hand and gave me a medallion of the Madonna (in Albanian called *medallion e Shenmeris*) and said, "Keep this medallion with you always, my child, as a reminder of God's blessings in your life."

The moment she touched me, I felt something rush through every vein of my body. It felt as if I were being embraced by my grandmother. And I felt power surge into me. My eyes must have been sparkling with excitement. The smile I returned to Mother Teresa came from deep within my heart and was full of pure, innocent love.

I thanked Mother Teresa in Albanian: *"Faliminderit shumë."* Then I ran back through the crowd of people toward my grandparents' house

The medallion Mother Teresa gave me.

to tell my mother about what had happened. I was almost out of breath as I ran up the stairs and walked into the house.

"What's the matter with you, Laura?" my mother asked.

"Mami, mami! I just met a small, wrinkled old woman wrapped in a white sheet with blue lines. People called her *Nënë Teresa* and she chose me out of the whole crowd and gave me this medallion," I replied.

I opened my fist, which I had held tightly closed, and showed the medallion to my mother. I knew in my heart that it was a special treasure from above. "Mother Teresa said I was going to have a blessed future."

My mother's eyes filled with tears of joy.

"My love, I watched from the balcony while Mother Teresa gave this to you. That's because you are a very special little girl. Do you know, Laura, that this Mother Teresa you just met is the woman I dreamed about? Just as she gave me a handful of medallions in my dream, she gave you a medallion today in reality. Do you see, my love, that dreams can become reality?"

The medallion became one of the most precious gifts I have ever received, and I treasure it in my heart. After my experience with Mother Teresa, my mother often talked to me about this special woman of God: "Mother Teresa is a role model for many because she dedicates her life to helping the poorest of the poor all around the globe. She is a woman who faces the harshest types of human misery and yet pours out unconditional love to help the sickest people survive. Mother Teresa is an example for the whole world of unconditional love. She loves everyone no matter who they are. One of those people was you, Laura."

Photo my mother has of Mother Teresa with a sick child in her arms.

As the years progressed, and after learning more about Mother Teresa, I felt even more blessed to have been the first person that day to have been touched by a such an exceptional person.

Laura's Reflection on *A Treasure from Above*

Being invited by Mother Teresa out of the huge crowd in Tirana, Albania, to go to her so she could hand me a precious gift, the silver medallion, has taught me to trust God when He is speaking to me. That day when Mother Teresa pointed to me and chose me out of everyone else in the crowd, my first thought was to not trust a stranger. But I heard a small quite voice speak to me inwardly, assuring me that I could fully trust this woman, that she was extraordinary.

I believe God was directly speaking to me and guiding my actions. This taught me that we should trust our instincts when we feel God's presence within us. If we feel that God is directing us toward a good, positive action, we should trust that it is the correct action to take. This is not to say we should make drastic life decisions merely on instinct without receiving advice from trusted mentors.

This experience changed my life forever. It taught me that the greatest treasures in life come in small packages. The moment I received the silver medallion from Mother Teresa, even without knowing who Mother Teresa was, I cherished it. I held on to it and would not let go, even though I did not fully understand its meaning. God has since impressed upon my heart that the silver medallion should be cherished as a reminder that He is ultimately in control of my destiny.

People benefit from cherishing some things in their hearts even if they are tiny, such as a wedding ring. Some of you may cherish, no matter how small, a special lock, pendant, or jewel inherited or gifted from an important person in your life. Such gifts are worth far more than any monetary value they may be assigned.

Study Guide Companion

❖ If you feel a strong spiritual leading in your life to make a particular decision, how would you know that you are making the right choice?

❖ Think of a beloved public figure. What would you do if you saw that person directly in front of you? What would you say?

❖ What do you consider the greatest gift you have received in your life? Explain.

CHAPTER 2
A FAMILY FILLED WITH LOVE

My family and I come from Albania, a small, mountainous country in the Balkan peninsula, located to the north of Greece and south of Montenegro and Kosovo. Albania has numerous pristine beaches along the Adriatic and Ionian coastlines. Albania has a population of approximately 3 million people. Tirana is the nation's capital and largest city, followed by Durrës, my hometown, and Vlorë, my mother's birth town.

My family in Tirana, Albania, 1988.

Albania is a nation that was ruled by the Ottoman Empire for centuries; therefore, the Turkish influence is significant. Three religions are practiced in Albania: Catholicism, 30 percent; Orthodox Christianity, 10 percent, and Islam, 60 percent. There is an extraordinary religious tolerance among Albanians. Members of the same family sometimes belong to different religions and it is very common for two people from different religions to marry. I know several families in which one spouse is Muslim and the other is Catholic or Orthodox. But my grandparents were both Orthodox.

After World War II, Albania became a communist nation under its leader Enver Hoxha, but transitioned to democracy after 1990. During the majority of my childhood, Albania was a communist nation.

My greatest role model in life is my mother. My mother taught me from an early age that the most sacred thing in life is family and love.

My grandmother Aleksandra, with my mother's younger brother, Ilir, my mother's older brother, Maqo, and my grandfather, Lefter, with my mother in a family portrait in Tirana, Albania, 1955.

My mother, Marjeta, grew up in a family filled with love and laughter. Both her parents taught her how to love—how to cherish the love you receive and how to always give more love to people who are hungry for love. As Mother Teresa believed, the greatest hunger our world faces is the hunger for love. My mother's parents instilled this in their children. Her parents demonstrated how to be hospitable with everyone in their lives, whether rich or poor, young or old, close family friends or strangers.

My grandfather, Lefter, and my grandmother, Aleksandra, in their house in Tirana, Albania.

My grandmother, Aleksandra, taught my mother to always treat the poor with love, admiration, and respect—especially neighbors. My mother lived in "Café Flora," considered one of the most modern and wealthiest neighborhoods of Tirana, and the majority of the people living in her neighborhood were middle to upper class. Even so, there were a few lower-class people who lived there as well. Just like Mother Teresa, my grandmother recognized no boundaries. She loved and cared for all her neighbors, but it was the less fortunate and poor who touched her heart most.

My mother with some of her neighbors in Tirana, Albania, 1962.

One of my mother's fondest childhood memories is of her mother cooking a delicious meal and taking a huge platter of it to her poorest neighbors, a family with eight children. Because they were very poor, the family could only afford to buy peppers and bread. On a daily basis, they ate only fried peppers on pieces of rustic wheat bread. When my mother accompanied my grandmother while taking these neighbors a platter of food, she was happy to first immerse herself in their world by waiting in line with all the children to get a piece of bread with a fried pepper on it. She wanted the children to see that she was content with very little food just as they were. My mother was overjoyed when she saw the family sharing the food that her mother had prepared with such love. This feeling cannot be described because it lies so deeply within the heart. Even as a child my mother did not judge people, she simply loved them unconditionally.

My grandmother taught my mother valuable life goals and was my mother's greatest inspiration. She taught my mother to always help anyone who asks for help and to share our daily bread. My mother recalled my grandmother's words of wisdom:

> *"My dear daughter, if you eat in front of someone, don't ever start eating without offering to share it with others first. When they have food, you have food. You will feel much happier eating when you share with others. Always remember, my dear, never speak badly about people even if they are your worst enemies. You must*

love your enemies and turn them into your friends. Never speak about people unless you have nothing but good things to say about them. Most important, always love one another uncondi- tionally no matter what the situation is."

Just as Mother Teresa did, my grandmother believed that being unwanted, unloved, uncared for, and forgotten creates a much greater hunger, a much greater poverty than that of someone who has nothing to eat. Therefore, sharing our daily bread is not just about offering a person food but about feeding that person with love.

My grandmother talked to my mother continually about the impor- tance of daily prayer and having faith in God because it is only He who will lead us on the best path of life. My grandmother instilled these prin- ciples in my mother and my mother instilled them in me. I am the person I am today because of this godly heritage.

Let me tell you more about my family. My mother, Marjeta, grad- uated from the University of Tirana with a degree in the English and Albanian languages. During her university years and after graduating, my mother served as an interpreter for many foreign delegations that came from countries such as Australia, Malta, and France. She later became an English teacher in the Tirana School of Foreign Languages. After teaching there for three years, she became an English professor for post-university students in the Gjergj Kastrioti School in our hometown of Durrës.

My mother, Marjeta, as an interpreter and English teacher accompanying delegations from France, Malta, and Australia. Albania, 1971–1972.

My father, Frederik, graduated from Tirana University with a law degree and a philosophy degree. My father was a philosophy professor for about ten years at the Gjergj Kastrioti School, the same school where my mother taught. Later, for ten years he worked at the Port of Durrës with cargo trade ships traveling all around the world. After working at the port, my father became the chief of the air traffic control at the Tirana International Airport now named "Nënë Teresa International Airport," after our beloved Mother Teresa.

My father, Frederik, traveling in the cockpit on one of his business trips as the chief of the air traffic control at Tirana Airport.

My brother, Dritan, is seven years older than I am. My brother helped raise me and is very dear to my heart. Since my brother was seven years old when I was born, he was old enough to serve as my parents' little helper. He woke up at 5:00 a.m. every day to go out and buy fresh milk for me. He babysat me when my parents went to work. He fed me, changed me, and rocked me to sleep. My brother was a very mature seven-year-old. He sacrificed part of his childhood to take care of his little sister. He has always held a special place in my heart.

My father, Frederik; my brother, Dritan; my mother, Marjeta; and myself as a baby. Durrës, Albania, 1985.

My brother and me. Durrës, Albania, 1986.

The time came that I began to imitate my mother and my grandmother. When I was a child we lived in a neighborhood in Durrës with very poor families and had a lot of neighbors who were much less fortunate than we were. But, on a daily basis, that is where I loved to play. I felt at home with them. My mother always served them by taking delicious food to them and by providing them with clothes.

My mother as a teacher had a higher social status. Our neighbors respected her profession and also respected her amazing generosity. My mother felt what she was doing was very small. By befriending the poor, she demonstrated that she was a simple person who lived a simple life, so they would feel better that they, too, lived simple lives.

My mother taught me from the time I was very young that the people we should help the most are the elderly and children. She taught me this in a special way on birthdays. As a child, I counted down the seconds until my birthday, just as any child would. But I did not do it for selfish reasons but rather because of the anticipation of making all my little friends happy on my special day. selfish reasons but rather because of the anticipation of making all my little friends happy on my special day.

With my friends at my ninth birthday party at my house. Durrës, Albania.

My mother invited all the little girls in the neighborhood, approximately twenty-five of them, to our house for a birthday feast. Not only did she put together both a delicious lunch and dinner, but she also put a smile on every little girl's face as she showered her with surprise birthday presents from the birthday girl and her.

At my birthday parties we also planned special games and activities, such as talent competitions, to entertain our guests. My favorite was the "Tiny Miss Albania" pageant for all the little girls in the neighborhood. The girls would come dressed in princess gowns. Unlike how the official Miss Albania contest operated, where only one girl received the final prize, my mother had gifts for all the girls. These presents were dresses, tiaras, perfumes, hair accessories, dolls, and so on. When the girls left, they all had big smiles on their faces. I experienced many happy moments during my birthdays throughout my childhood.

My mother often told my brother and me: "As a child, I remember that in our home in Tirana, even if it was 8:00 p.m. and the doorbell would ring, my mother and father would welcome whoever it was with a smile, a smile filled with love. My mother would immediately prepare whatever food she had and put it out on the table to share with our guests. My father would entertain our guests by playing the mandolin and guitar in order to have a cheerful time together."

It was examples like this that taught my mother to do the same. Throughout my entire childhood, I recall that whenever our doorbell rang, my mother would welcome our guests with open arms. She would immediately put food on the table to share, just as she watched her mother do.

 I followed in my grandfather's footsteps, entertaining our guests by dancing, singing, or reciting poems. As soon as I started to talk, I became very sociable. One of my fondest memories as a toddler is of some family friends laughing because I asked the question: "Where is your Fredi?" As a baby, my father always said to me: "Come to Fredi! Come to Fredi!" Since Fredi was his name, I thought the word "Fredi" meant "father" in Albanian. When I asked our friends in my baby voice: "Where is your Fredi?" they all had a puzzled look on their face.

My brother, Dritan, age 6. Durrës, Albania.

My brother, Dritan, would do the same, but in a different way. He would take our guests' shoes and hide them and say: "You are not going anywhere tonight! You must sleep in our house! We are one big happy family!"

My parents taught us how to love one another as a family. Unconditional love is the true definition of a holy family.

Laura's Reflection on *A Family Filled with Love*

The experience of being raised in a family filled with love has taught me one of the greatest lessons of my life: to love unconditionally. I learned from a very young age that we must love everyone who crosses our paths, regardless of their social status, race, nationality, skin color, or religion. We are all made in God's image and we should treat all people equally.

Growing up in a diverse social-class neighborhood in Durrës, Albania, taught me to treat everyone the same, to respect everyone the same, to show appreciation to everyone in the same way, and to value them in the same way. I have applied this lesson throughout my life and it has become my lifelong goal. When I meet a person, I don't judge them because of their profession, race, nationality, or religion, I simply love that person for the person he or she is.

We should apply this theory of unconditional love to our lives, no matter the circumstances. We lose nothing by giving unconditional love, we only gain that same love in return. Even if there are people who refuse to receive our love, we have lost nothing because we will know that we tried. If anyone asks us for help to do a good thing, we should help when it will benefit them, even if our help goes unappreciated, because we are doing what God wants us to do, which is help and love one another.

Study Guide Companion

❖ What would you do if you were asked to help a stranger?

❖ How do you treat someone who is completely different from you?

❖ What is your definition of unconditional love? Do you consider unconditional love something you should give only to your family?

❖ Do you feel it is important to imitate family, friends, or other people who do good deeds?

❖ Who are your role models? Why did you select them?

❖ The Bible provides many role models. Read 1 Corinthians 11:1 and Ephesians 5:1–2.

CHAPTER 3
AN UNEXPECTED KNOCK

I will never forget September 23, 1991, as long as I live. That day was special because it was my brother's birthday and he turned thirteen years old. Along with the excitement of a birthday celebration, there was an unexpected knock at the door. Standing there was my mother's best friend, whose son was a former English student of my mother's. I was filled with excitement when I heard her give my mother the happiest news.

"Marjeta, the Sisters of Mother Teresa are asking that you come to teach them the Albanian and English languages! They request that you go today to the House of Missionaries of Charity."

Immediately my mother thought this reminded her of the miracle births of her children: "God is requiring my duty this day." She wanted to take on this new responsibility even though it would add to her usual teaching schedule, which was then three hours a day in the afternoons at the Gjergj Kastrioti school with post-university students.

Sister Clarisse and my brother Dritan at the House of Missionaries of Charity in Durrës, Albania in 1991.

After my brother's birthday party ended, my mother took both my brother and me by the hand and we went to the House of Missionaries of

Charity in Durrës. We had a pleasant twenty-minute walk along the beach boulevard to get to the House of Missionaries of Charity. This would be my mother's daily walk to teach the Sisters of Mother Teresa. gates of the convent opened and we were welcomed inside. There I was, a little six-year-old girl, walking through a convent with walls and ceilings covered with beautiful religious icons from all over the world.

The Sisters of Mother Teresa came to Albania to help house, feed, and care for the sick and the poorest of the poor.

Sister Clarisse waiving at the people inside the mini-van of the Missionaries of Charity in Durrës, Albania.

At first I thought I was dreaming as I was greeted by one hundred Sisters in white and blue saris, dressed exactly like Mother Teresa. But then I realized I was awake and this was indeed very real. The Superior, Sister Clarisse, led us to a little chapel to where a crowd of Sisters joyfully followed us. I tried to hide behind my mother but found myself surrounded by humble faces—all smiling at me—and again I realized this was not a dream.

My mother was overcome with emotion. She felt honored to accept whatever the Sisters requested of her. At that moment the words of her beloved mother and father were ringing in her ears: "Our dear daughter, you should always help the people as much as you can when they need help and you should never do wrong to anyone. You should love everyone unconditionally." Little did my mother know that the values my grandparents had instilled in her were going to be put into action in this new situation.

Sister Clarisse started by introducing herself and the other Sisters: "Good afternoon, Professor Marjeta Qirko. I am Sister Clarisse, the Superior in charge of the Sisters of the Missionaries of Charity in Albania."

She proudly continued: "Today we have the honor and privilege to have with us the famous Professor Marjeta Qirko. We are told she is one of the best English teachers in Albania."

Turning to my mother she said, "We were referred to you by Mrs. Dungu, whose son excels in English thanks to you. Mrs. Dungu told us that if we were looking for absolute success in working with the Albanian language, there is only one professor she highly recommends: Mrs. Marjeta Qirko."

My mother's eyes shone with pride.

Sister Clarisse continued: "Marjeta, we would be honored if you could teach us both the Albanian and English languages to prepare two different groups of Sisters. One group will be the Albanian girls coming from the north to be trained to go to the Vatican City. You would be teaching these girls English, because they are on their way to English-speaking countries such as India, England, and Australia.

"The other group consists of Sisters from eighty-one different countries. You would be teaching these Sisters Albanian because they need to communicate when they come to Albania for retreats and with Albanian Sisters in other countries."

When my mother heard this request, she immediately thought about how extremely difficult this was going to be. She knew that teaching English to the young women from northern Albania was going to be a great challenge because the living conditions there were not good. Many of these girls would come with very little to no educational background—most would be illiterate. She would have to teach them basic Albanian grammar before embarking on the English language.

Sister Clarisse continued: "Marjeta, to fulfill our greatest desire, it is crucial that all our Sisters learn the Albanian language. Since we are in Mother Teresa's homeland, we would love nothing more than to make her proud upon her next visit to Albania by being able to fully communicate with her in her own language.

"We have been told that you teach postgraduate courses every afternoon at the Gjergj Kastrioti school. Our request is that you come here to the House of Missionaries of Charity in Durrës every day for four to five hours in the morning for a three-year period to teach our Sisters. We understand the complexity and the difficulty of this job and are willing to negotiate whatever type of contract you would sign. What do you think is best for you, Marjeta?"

Overwhelmed with joy, my mother stood up and said, "I feel very happy that I am in a House of Charity. I more than gladly accept this job and will do it with pleasure, even though it will be extremely difficult and challenging, but with one condition."

Sister Clarisse stared deeply into my mother's eyes and said, "Whatever your condition is, we will accept it with pleasure."

My mother amazed the Sisters with her reply: "At this moment I am in the House of Charity of my greatest heroine, the beloved Mother Teresa. Therefore, I will dedicate all my work for charity just as she has dedicated all her work for charity. I want to follow Mother Teresa's example today and always. I am honored to do it free of charge."

When the Sisters heard my mother's words, they were flabbergasted and responded with "God will bless you and be with you always!" They could not believe what she was saying. "In our eyes you are truly a blessed woman!" Out of the 365 homes they had around the world, the first thing each teacher demanded was always a full, paying contract.

Sister Clarisse stood up, touched my mother's forehead, and said, "God bless you! God will be with you! God bless your family!"

Sister Clarisse stood up, touched my mother's forehead, and said, "God bless you! God will be with you! God bless your family!"

When Sister Clarisse touched my mother's forehead, my mother felt as if God was touching her and personally sending her on the mission of a lifetime. As I looked at my mother, I saw tears of joy running down my mother's cheeks and the happiest smile I had ever seen on her precious face.

All the Sisters stood up and started clapping and cheering: "Professor Marjeta! Professor Marjeta! Professor Marjeta!"

Each Sister waited her turn to greet my mother as if she were an angel. From a child's perspective this was surreal. Memories of meeting Mother Teresa in the center of a crowd in Tirana flashed across my memory and I felt proud of my mother in the same way as when I saw Mother Teresa the day she chose me from the crowd and gave me the silver medallion and the people were cheering her name: *"Nënë Teresa! Nënë Teresa!"* And now the Sisters were cheering my mother's name: "Professor Marjeta! Professor Marjeta!"

The Sisters saw us off with special prayers in their own languages, prayers that have truly changed both my mother's and my life forever.

Laura's Reflection of *An Unexpected Knock*

Seeing my mother invited on the journey of a lifetime—teaching the Sisters of Mother Teresa—taught me that the best things in life come when you are not expecting them. It also taught me that we should follow our hearts to guide our actions when choosing between two good possibilities. The Sisters of Mother Teresa came to our house in Durrës, Albania, to give my mother the life-changing news that they wanted her to teach them Albanian and English when my mother least expected it. My mother not only rose to the challenge, but she also followed her heart when it told her to accept this mission from God but to accept it with one condition: she would do it free of charge. This taught me that there is nothing better in life than setting examples of charity.

Since that day, I have applied this maxim to my life in many ways. For example, now that I am a foreign language teacher just like my mother, whenever a student needs tutoring, I offer to do it on one condition: the tutoring will be done free of charge. It also brings me great happiness to work for charity as an interpreter around the world. I feel that, when I am working for a good organization, the salary they would have given me will be used toward projects that can better the community.

We should all try to perform acts of charity, no matter how rich or poor we might be, no matter what our profession. The joy from doing a special deed for charity is worth all the money in the world. People should not do jobs just for the money involved. Whenever possible, people should work at jobs they are passionate about and do them for the right reasons.

For example, being a teacher, I can tell you that teachers should do their jobs not only to earn salaries, but also, and more important, for the benefit of their students. Teaching students with love and passion and trying to make a difference in their lives is what makes a teacher's day.

We cannot live happily unless we know we are making a difference in someone's life. Changing people's lives by acts of charity will change our lives and our conception of the world we are living in. Mother Teresa taught that you can change a person's life even if you are very poor—just by a smile.

Study Guide Companion

❖ At the end of the day, do you rejoice more from making money or how you made a difference in someone's life?

❖ If you were handed the job of a lifetime, would you think of accepting it not just for the money, but for the joy it would bring you?

❖ What are some acts of charity you have done for your family, friends, or strangers?

❖ The apostle Paul had every right to take a salary from those he taught, but he refused and worked as a tentmaker, probably into the late hours of the night—a real sacrifice. He was more concerned about the spiritual growth of his students than a paycheck. Read Acts 18:3 and 1 Corinthians 9:11–18.

CHAPTER 4
SET ON A MISSION

You will not be surprised that with a mother such as mine, I would one day also become a language teacher.

My mother and I in our house in Durrës, Albania in 1991, the year she started teaching the Sisters of Mother Teresa.

The clock struck 6:00 a.m., and my mother woke up to what would be one of the most unforgettable days of her life. I heard her whispering as she kissed me to wake me up. "Laura, today is the big day when our lives will change forever. Today I will begin the most special mission of my life. Today I am going to the House of the Missionaries of Charity. It is my first day teaching the Sisters of Mother Teresa from all around the world."

I jumped out of bed full of excitement and said, "Yes, Mami, I wish you the best success!"

There was little time for chatting. I gave her a kiss on the cheek as she prepared to enter again the majestic gates of the convent on her special mission from God.

My mother left every morning to arrive at eight o'clock at the House of Missionaries of Charity to teach the Sisters. She would take me with her since I was free in the mornings. In Albania, schools had a morning session and an afternoon session. My mother as a teacher and I as a student attended the afternoon sessions. This schedule allowed me to go to the convent every day with my mother.

My mother was welcomed by twenty Sisters. Some of the Sisters were happy, some were nervous, some were shy. Some were extremely enthusiastic at the thought of learning the difficult Albanian language. None of the Sisters knew what approach my mother was going to use in teaching them. Because most of them did not speak much English or Albanian, my mother used her multilingual skills to communicate with the Sisters as they introduced themselves in English by stating their names and where they came from.

For example: "My name is Sister Nirmala and I come from India."

After my mother listened to the Sisters' introductions, it was her turn to introduce herself in English. With the Sisters sitting in a huge hall overlooking the sea, my mother stood up and said, "Good morning, dear Sisters. My name is Marjeta Qirko and I am an English teacher here in Durrës. I have graduated from Tirana University with a degree in the English and Albanian languages. I have been teaching English for the past twenty-eight years. Currently I am teaching English at Gjergj Kastrioti school in the afternoons. It is my honor and privilege to be here among you today and, from this moment, to be able to call you all my dear students.

"Teaching you these languages, especially the Albanian language, will be extremely difficult, but I will try to make it most beneficial for each and every one of you. I am a great believer in differentiated instructions. I will tell you now that I will be extremely strict in teaching you these languages as fast as possible in order for you to communicate with the Albanian people and fulfill your missions. I believe that when one has deep faith in God, one never gives up. Therefore, I will never give up and I encourage each one of you to never give up as well. It will take a lot of time and dedication on both my part and your parts but we will gladly do it together in the name of our Lord. Amen!"

During her lessons, my mother would often see the Sisters looking at one another with consternation over the difficulty of learning the Albanian language. But after my mother reassured them about how successful they would be with her help, they smiled as hope entered their hearts. The message conveyed was that just as she, their teacher, was courageous, they, too, must be courageous. Later when I became a teacher, I followed my mother's example by encouraging hope and a future for my students.

My mother explained to me on the way home from the convent: "In front of me, in those first moments of teaching the Sisters today, appeared a figure who reminded me of Jesus. Whether it was a vision or a dream I do not know, but I felt in my heart of hearts His approval. This gave me strength and courage to face any obstacle that would come my way. I thanked God and felt blessed to have His approval."

***

My mother had two groups to teach: a large group consisting of the Sisters from all around the world who were learning Albanian to communicate with the Albanian people, and a smaller group consisting of the young women from northern Albania who were learning English to travel to English-speaking nations around the world. My mother taught the large group Albanian in a very big hall in the convent overlooking the Adriatic Sea and she taught the smaller group English in the dining hall.

My mother began teaching the Sisters the Albanian language, which was so hard for the Sisters coming from different countries. For instance, the Albanian language contains thirty-six letters in the alphabet and has many different prefixes and suffixes. The Sisters tried their best to comprehend this difficult language. My mother devoted her time to helping them, just as she had promised them since the very first day. She patiently corrected every single letter they wrote and every single word they spoke.

When some of the Sisters were absent because of other duties, my mother wrote down everything they missed in detail to help them catch up and prepare for the next day. She handwrote the day's lesson for each of the Sisters who were on retreat.

What surprised my mother the most was the Sisters' dedication to learning the Albanian language. This was the way they were going to carry on with their missions. They knew they needed to speak the people's language as they visited them in their homes, helped families in need with babies, small children, or elderly people living with them.

My mother created and practiced different types of dialogues with the Sisters, pretending she was an Albanian with whom they were having real-life conversations. She also helped them individually grasp the Albanian language better and faster. From the very beginning she encouraged them by saying: "With the help of God, you can do it. Never fear making mistakes. You can't learn a language without making mistakes. I will follow you around when you are talking to Albanian people so I can see how to help you."

When my mother saw how much the Sisters had progressed in speaking Albanian, she was proud that, with her hard work and dedication and with their preparation and determination, they had achieved their goal.

**

My mother also had the second group of Sisters, which consisted of the Albanian girls coming from the northern part of Albania who were going to learn English in order to go to Rome and serve as nuns in Vatican City. It was a real challenge for my mother to teach these young women. Most of them had had very little schooling in the northern villages of Albania where they came from.

In the mountains, a school could be two or three hours walking distance from their homes. Because the climate is bitter cold and filled with snow and ice, schooling was not an option for most of these girls. The few that had gone to school, had attended for only short periods of time, learning very little reading and writing skills. Because of this, my mother used to teach them first the correct Albanian grammar and then the English language.

With my mother's enduring patience and the Sisters' determination, they did their best, succeeded in learning the English language, and went to Rome to continue their mission. My mother was very touched when they sent her a thank-you card, blessing her for everything she did for them. Receiving those beautiful words of gratitude was the best blessing my mother could ever receive.

The Sisters of Mother Teresa were special not only to us, but to all Albanians because they helped with the basic struggles of life, whether it was with family, food, clothing, or spiritual or medical intervention. They provided heartfelt aid to all poorest of the poor in Albania and all around the world, always free of charge. It was exactly this humanitarian reason why my mother was the happiest person during her mission of teaching the Albanian and English languages for three years free of charge.

***

Every day she took my little hand as we walked to the House of Missionaries of Charity and I stood with her all morning, listening as she taught the Sisters. Those three years were the most beautiful times I can remember as a child because they taught me so much about helping one another in every way we are able to. I observed how to be kind to others, how to share with others, how to appreciate others, and, most important, how to love someone.

Did I just sit quietly all those hours while my mother was teaching language skills? No. I was allowed to visit the orphanage of the House of Missionaries of Charity, which was on the same grounds. I loved to take care of the little babies, helping to feed them or simply playing with them, showing them love. I got especially attached to a beautiful baby boy named Ignazio. Every day he was the first person I would see and the last one I would say goodbye to.

During those three years my entire family was involved in this mission from God. My brother Dritan, a young teenager at the time, dedicated his life to helping the Missionaries of Charity fulfill their goals. Only fourteen years old, he accompanied the Sisters from the north to the south of Albania where they brought supplies to help the poor families. My brother was more mature than most boys his age and excelled in languages. He served as an interpreter for the Sisters, translating from English into Albanian and from Italian to Albanian.

My brother Dritan accompaning Monsignor, the priest from the Catholic church in Durrës, Albania.

Helping in this way changed Dritan's life forever as he became very devoted to the Catholic religion, especially the Catholic Church in Durrës. For many years he served as an altar boy and helped priests from all over the world. My brother's work and dedication paid off in a special way: he was baptized on March 27, 1993, in Durrës, Albania, at the Shtëpia Motrave, the House of Missionaries of Charity, in the presence of the Sisters of Mother Teresa.

You may wonder why he wasn't baptized as a baby. During the time he was a baby, in Albania the Church was not allowed to baptize in the parish.

My brother with Sister Clarisse and the other children from Durrës on his baptism day.

My brother did not know that the day he was baptized was the first day of what would be a lifelong connection with Mother Teresa.

My father, Frederik, also devoted time to helping in this mission. At that time he was the chief of the air traffic control in Tirana Airport. He helped the Missionaries of Charity when they would arrive at the airport. He would personally walk up to the plane and accompany them through customs, giving them the highest priority. He would help accommodate whatever goods they brought for the Albanian community. He also helped with the language barrier since he spoke English quite well.

One day Sister Clarisse asked my mother: "Dear Professor Marjeta, there is a priest from Malta who is coming with a few of his missionaries. Would it be all right with the Qirko family if we hosted him in your house as your guest for three or four days?"

My mother replied, "With the greatest pleasure we will accept them as if they were a part of the family."

My mother thought about how Mother Teresa said to always open up the door and welcome guests when they need a place to stay.

We helped the priest and his missionaries with everything they needed to make their mission as successful as possible. My mother and my brother served as his personal translators, accompanying the missionaries everywhere in Albania, visiting some of the poorest families. When we welcomed the missionaries to our house, my mother was always very hospitable and cooked delicious Albanian dishes for them.

They appreciated our help so much that in order to show their deep appreciation and gratitude, they filmed a documentary about their experiences in Albania in which they highlighted my family's involvement and dedication in this mission. By directly helping them, we were indirectly helping God.

Laura's Reflection on *Set on a Mission*

The experience of working on a mission from God by working with the Sisters of Mother Teresa and other dedicated Christians, taught me there is nothing better to give in this life than service to our brothers and sisters. First of all, witnessing my mother's dedication in teaching the Sisters taught me to appreciate and fall in love with teaching. It taught me to always do my best to encourage students to learn to the best of their abilities. It taught me to never give up on students no matter how difficult the challenge of teaching them might be. It taught me to always put students first and push them to their limits in order to see them succeed.

Watching the progress the Sisters made in learning the Albanian language and the pride in my mother's eyes when they achieved this taught me the beauty of seeing your hard work pay off in the best way possible. We should always encourage one another to do our best to succeed in whatever we are trying to do. By encouraging and supporting one another, we will live in a happier and prouder world.

Witnessing my brother accompany the Missionaries of Charity and interpreting for them inspired me to do the same, especially since he did so at such a young age. Seeing his devotion and dedication to helping the poor by doing good deeds served as a great inspiration for me. I began applying this while I was a child in the House of Missionaries of Charity in Durrës by helping with the babies in the orphanage.

Watching my parents' hospitality of opening our home and welcoming the visiting priests and brothers of the Missionaries of Charity as part of the family taught me the lesson that we should always welcome people into our homes and make our homes safe, comfortable, and blessed places for them to visit. As an adult, I have always had the heart to open our house to guests from all around the world. I want to give them the best experience possible during their stay with us. I want them to feel as if they are part of the family and that our home is their home.

We should always keep our doors open to welcome people who are in need or who are dear to our hearts. By taking care of them, we are honoring God, since all the people in the world are God's children. Read how Jesus responded to the little children (Luke 18:16).

Study Guide Companion

❖ Would you ever open up your home to a stranger and make him or her feel like family? Read Hebrews 13:2.

❖ What would you consider the best gift we can give one another?

❖ If God gave you a specific mission, could you dedicate your life to it?

CHAPTER 5
A MIRACLE FROM ABOVE

One of the most unforgettable times of my youth is when I experienced a personal supernatural healing. The Sisters of Mother Teresa truly blessed me and at one point it was this blessing that saved my life.

My mother and I walking to the House of Missionaries of Charity in Durrës, Albania in 1993.

One day before my mother and I went to the House of the Missionaries of Charity, we visited some friends. They talked about how beautiful I was and what a good little girl I was for going with my mother every day when she taught the Sisters. As my mother and I were walking to go to the House of Missionaries of Charity, I felt very lightheaded. As we approached the convent, it got worse. Not to worry my mother, I did not say a word to her about how I was feeling.

When we arrived, I went to see Ignazio, an orphan whom I loved dearly. My mother had gone to the Chapel to teach the Sisters. It felt like the room was spinning upside down. The objects in the room seemed to fade. At this point, I decided to go to my mother and tell her what was happening.

Walking from one room to another, cold chills allover my small body, I spotted a railing near the wall. The last thing I remember is holding on to that railing and calling out for my mother. At that instant, everything went black and I fainted.

Hearing my fall, everyone rushed out of the rooms to see what had happened. They were terrified to find me on the floor. My mother tried to wake me. The Sisters carried me to their Prayer Room where they recited a special prayer for me:

"Our dear Lord, please protect and save this little girl from any harm. For she is one of the sweetest and most loving girls we know who dedicates her time to our community, coming here with her mother, as she teaches us the Albanian and English languages. Little Laura accompanies her mother and patiently waits for her four to five hours every day. She spends those hours caring for and loving our dear children in the orphanage even though she is a young child herself. Please, we pray to you our Lord to make her well. Amen!"

As the Sisters prayed for my recovery, I began to hear what was going on and opened my eyes little by little. They gave me holy water with sugar to drink, and as soon as I took one sip, I felt as if nothing had happened at all.

I then got up on my feet, filled with energy, and played all day long. As I look back upon this amazing experience in my life, I recognize the protecting hand of God over me and am reminded of the words of Mother Teresa: "Keep this medallion with you always, my child, as a reminder of God's blessings in your life." For me, this is a true miracle from above.

The bottle filled with the holy water that the Sisters gave me that day in Durrës, Albania.

Laura's Reflection on *A Miracle from Above*

The experience of being healed through prayer to God by the Sisters of Mother Teresa taught me to believe in miracles. I had never experienced a healing miracle before the day the Sisters prayed for me and blessed me with the holy water. I now believe the power of praying to God is the strongest power we possess. We must always pray to God to help us, not only in times of blessing, but in our weakest moments as well. We must have faith that God is our healer who can make miracles occur. The day I passed out on the floor in the House of the Missionaries of Charity, the Sister's prayers went straight to God's ears and He revived me.

Study Guide Companion

❖ Have you ever experienced a miraculous event in your life or in the life of somebody you know?

❖ Do you believe God can heal you or somebody you know through prayer?

❖ Do you fear the worst at your weakest moment? If so what helps you rise back up?

CHAPTER 6
A BIG SURPRISE

April 1994 was a special month in Albania. Mother Teresa came for what would become one of her last visits to her beloved country. This trip was dear to her heart because it was dedicated to helping the people of her beloved motherland.

She came to witness the charity of her Sisters in the Albanian community. Among the many visits she made that month from the north to the south of Albania, her primary destination was Durrës, where her first stop was the House of the Missionaries of Charity.

What shocked Mother Teresa upon arriving in Durrës was how well the Sisters were communicating in Albanian with the Albanian people. She was very proud of this.

Mother Teresa was so impressed with them that the first thing she asked Sister Clarisse was: "Who is your teacher who has done such a phenomenal job? Tell her and her family to come here at 10:00 a.m. tomorrow because I want to meet her. I have to bless her for what she has done for us. She has not only helped our community (the Sisters of the Missionaries of Charity) but also all of the larger Albanian community as well. This woman is truly wonderful and I am honored to give her and her family a special private blessing."

Upon hearing Mother Teresa's request, Sister Clarisse notified my mother about the once-in-a-lifetime opportunity of meeting and being blessed by Mother Teresa.

Sister Clarisse said to my mother: "Professor Marjeta I have great news for you. As you very well know, our beloved Mother Teresa is here in Durrës and was extremely proud to see the Sisters communicating with the Albanian community in Albanian due to the phenomenal job you have done with our Sisters. She requested your presence tomorrow at 10:00 a.m. for a private visit with you, your husband, Frederick, your son, Dritan, and your daughter, Laura. She would like to bestow her blessing upon you and your family for all the hard work and dedication you have done. Due to the fact that this is going to be a very private and heartfelt meeting, there is no photography allowed. You must all be here tomorrow morning."

My family in April of 1994 right before the blessing with Mother Teresa. My mother Marjeta, my father Frederik, my brother Dritan and myself in Durrës, Albania.

My mother could not believe her ears. Her eyes, filled with tears of joy, seemed to reflect deep gratitude to God who had sent this special saint to bless her and her family in this way.

My mother replied to Sister Clarisse: "Sister Clarisse, this is a great privilege and honor to meet the extraordinary woman who is and will always continue to be my greatest human role model and hero."

This news touched all of our hearts deeply. We knew our lives were going to change the moment we met Mother Teresa.

I felt I truly was the most special girl in the world to have the privilege of not only meeting Mother Teresa for the second time, but also by being personally blessed by her. There are thousands of people who dream of just touching Mother Teresa for a second, and I was given the opportunity to spend quality time with her and receive a personal blessing from her. I counted the seconds until my meeting with Mother Teresa.

Laura's Reflection on *A Big Surprise*

The experience of being given an opportunity to meet a woman such as Mother Teresa taught me to increase my faith in God, for He can make our biggest dreams a reality. Meeting Mother Teresa was a dream of my entire family, just as it was for everyone in Albania. The blessing of meeting with Mother Teresa privately made me believe that if we give generously, we will receive in an even more wonderful way. My mother gave her time and dedication to teaching the Sisters of Mother Teresa free of charge for three years and God repaid her by having her receive a blessing from Mother Teresa herself. This taught me that every good deed in life is always paid back when you least expect it. As God sees you doing a good deed, He always remembers, and one day your good deed will be rewarded in an extraordinary way.

Study Guide Companion

- ❖ Do you believe that all good deeds one does are repaid in one way or another?

- ❖ If you give of yourself, do you believe you will receive?

- ❖ Do we give to get or do we give to bless others?

- ❖ Do we believe that God sees all of our good works and is faithful to reward us?

- ❖ Read Hebrews 11:6 and James 2:14, 26.

CHAPTER 7
AN HOUR WITH MOTHER TERESA

The night before the meeting with Mother Teresa was one of the longest of our lives. As each minute ticked by, our hearts raced. We thought about how big God is that He gave us the opportunity of making our dream a reality by meeting this extraordinary woman in a private meeting planned just for our family. We thanked God as we counted down each minute until 10:00 a.m., the time set for us to arrive at the convent to meet the beloved Mother Teresa.

My family in April 1994 right before the blessing with Mother Teresa. My brother, Dritan, my father, Frederik, myself, and my mother, Marjeta. Durrës, Albania.

Sister Clarisse led us up to the second floor, where all the Sisters and Mother Teresa were waiting for us. I squeezed my mother's hand as my family and I waited for the doors to open and for Mother Teresa to welcome us inside.

The room overlooked the Adriatic Sea. It was a beautiful spring morning, **with the birds chirping as the soft breeze swept through the palm trees. T**he Sisters were kneeling in prayer as the doors opened for us to walk inside and the most beautiful woman of God stood right in front of us.

The Sisters of Mother Teresa kneeling during a prayer to Jesus Christ.

There was Mother Teresa in her famous blue and white sari, barefoot as usual. Next to her was her private secretary, a tall blond woman, writing down what was said.

My eyes once again met those of the little old woman. Mother Teresa embraced me and kissed my cheek. The moment she touched me, I felt something like electricity rush through my body. I saw my mother's face light up as this holy woman, who dedicated her life to helping the poorest of the poor, embraced and kissed her, my father, and my brother. When Mother Teresa shook my mother's hand and kissed her on the cheek, my mother also felt a strong power radiate from her head to her toes.

Mother Teresa said, "Dear Marjeta, it is my great honor and privilege to have the blessing from our dear Lord to meet such an exceptional woman. Please forgive me because I have forgotten the Albanian language; therefore, we will speak in English. Please come sit by my side."

My mother held back tears as she sat down by Mother Teresa. The Sisters looked at my mother with the great pride, admiration, appreciation, and honor.

And then my mother began to speak: "First of all, Mother Teresa, I am truly honored to be standing in your presence because I am standing next to my heroine. You have been a role model for me and have inspired me to become the woman I am proud to be today. You are not only an inspiration for me but for millions and millions of people all around the world. Deep in my soul, I feel that God has given me a special blessing by sending you into our lives. In my eyes, Mother Teresa, you truly define the words noble humanitarian. Everything you have done during the past years has made you into the exceptional woman the world knows you to be today.

"You have gone from being a geography teacher to being the most famous and best-loved humanitarian in the world. You have dedicated your life to helping the poorest of the poor, the sickest of the sick, and to bettering the harshest human misery this world is currently facing.

"Please allow me to share with you two examples that sum up your noble character. Last night we saw a film dedicated to you, Mother Teresa. One particular scene brought tears to my eyes: when you hold the hand of a poor, abandoned old man who was lying on the pavement while worms sucked his blood and bit his flesh. In a dying voice, he asked you: 'Why are you helping me?' and your simple, noble answer was: 'Because I love you.' Mother Teresa, you really love people unconditionally as human beings because in your eyes they are all the children of God no matter what color, what race, what nationality, or what social status they possess.

"The scene in the movie that impressed me even more is when you come out of the Red Cross minivan in the Middle East, all the people surrounding you, and you say: 'I am not interested in any political parties, I am only interested in the common people.' This, Mother Teresa, illustrates the strong, passionate love you possess for all human beings."

Mother Teresa was brought to tears by my mother's words and continued squeezing my mother's hands. Then Mother Teresa said, "First of all, my dear Marjeta, you have touched me with your generous words. What has truly impressed me the most is that you have understood my message thoroughly and have taken action because of it. My Sisters have told me that you have enjoyed teaching them how to correctly speak the Albanian language, because your goal was for each of them to learn to speak well. I know that the Albanian language is very difficult. But with your patience and dedication you tried to make it easier to grasp the concepts of the language itself and to perfect these concepts by constantly practicing the language with the Albanian people.

"You have turned what was once a challenge for the Sisters into an everyday enjoyment. Above all, you didn't accept any money for teaching them four or five hours every day for so many years. This truly impresses me because out of the hundreds of homes that we have all around the world, the first thing each teacher demands is to sign a contract. I have a question for you, my dear. Why did you do all that work free of charge?"

My mother noticed the Sisters staring at her, eagerly awaiting her response.

My mother said, "It is very simple, Mother Teresa. You dedicate your life to the poorest of the poor and do everything for charity, so I am following in your footsteps and setting the best example for other people who are not in your community. I did it for charity too."

Mother Teresa stood up and placed her hands on my mother's forehead, saying, "God bless you and be with you! God will bless you in the future and I am laying my hands on you and asking the Lord to give you His healing touch, which is a gift from God that you might share it with the others."

While Mother Teresa talked to my mother, I listened to every golden word that came out of her mouth. Here are some of her parting words: "My dear Marjeta, since you have done something so special for us, I want to do something special for you. I will teach you a special prayer just for you."

My mother immediately said, "I feel so happy, Mother Teresa, because I know what this prayer will be about. It will stress the importance of forgiving people, sharing our daily bread with each other, and, above all, loving each other unconditionally as fellow human beings."

"That is exactly what it is about!" said Mother Teresa.

And my mother then shared another dream of hers. "Mother Teresa, today I am teaching the students in Albania but God knows possibly in the future I will teach students from all around the world and I will always spread your message of sharing and forgiveness to everyone I meet from this day forward."

Mother Teresa stood up and held my mother's hands tightly while she prayed: "I am holding your hands and asking the Lord to use these hands to bless and bring God's healing touch to people everywhere. Our dear Lord, Jesus Christ, please bless this woman I have in my presence. Always bestow upon her lots of good health and good fortune. Lead her to the most successful path in life for her. Fulfill her wishes as she has fulfilled ours. Always guide and protect her and make miracles come true for her and her dear family. I thank You, Lord, for allowing me to bless this wonderful woman today and always. In Your precious name, amen."

After this prayer, Mother Teresa came to each of us, starting with my mother, me, my brother, and then my father, putting her hands on our foreheads as she blessed us. When she touched me, I felt as if I were being touched by the hand of God. As a family we experienced a special spiritual connection with Mother Teresa and an eternal bond.

I realized that even though these events were so unusual, being in Mother Teresa's presence put me at ease because she was such a simple woman with such a noble heart. Every time she embraced me, I felt as if I was receiving a warm hug from my own grandmother instead of from an important public figure. Her holy and chaste behavior radiated throughout the room just like the time I saw her in the crowd in Tirana, only this time it was different because it was a private blessing.

What grabbed my attention was the simplicity of this woman. She was barefoot. To me this showed that she was a simple woman who considered herself like the poor, as she is. The contributions to her ministry go only to the poor. The Sisters themselves live in poverty and in India they don't even have toilet paper. This is to be in solidarity with the poorest of the poor.

Mother Teresa's voice was so sweet! Every time she opened her mouth it felt as if a bird was serenading you with a beautiful, valuable song. Among the many words we heard that day, there were three words that stuck out to me: help, share, and forgive.

The day Mother Teresa blessed us, she showered us with many special gifts. She gave my mother a large cross, which we have today, hanging in our living room. This cross acts as a reminder that we must look to Jesus who is the Author and Finisher of our faith. Whether we are facing rough times or good times, we pray to Jesus and it immediately brings light and hope to our day.

The cross of St. Francis of Assisi that Mother Teresa gave us the day of our blessing.

As Mother Teresa kissed me goodbye, she whispered in my ear: "My dear little Laura, remember to always help others, and never forget to share."

She handed me a huge red teddy bear with *"Buona Fortuna"* written on it, which in Italian means "good fortune." She then gave me a huge box, weighing about ten pounds. At first we had absolutely no idea what could be in this large box, but after we got home we discovered it was one giant, chocolate blessing.

Laura's Reflection on *An Hour with Mother Teresa*

Meeting Mother Teresa for the second time in my young life and receiving a private blessing with my family inspired me to become the woman I am today. Being blessed by Mother Teresa taught me how sacred and noble a humanitarian can be. Mother Teresa instilled lifelong goals in me: to always help people, share with people, and love people.

Mother Teresa taught and inspired me to become a noble humanitarian all over the world, just as she was. I dedicated my life to helping people from every nation, from every religion, from every race. Mother Teresa helped me see that we must not discriminate against people, but we must embrace all people, as we are all made in the image of God. An important message to spread in our world today is to pursue peace with all men, as well as to pursue holiness. A day is coming when God will wipe away every tear from our eyes, and there will be no more death or mourning or crying or pain, for the former things have passed away. As a family, we recognized the hour we spent with Mother Teresa would change the course of our lives forever.

Study Guide Companion

❖ What is your definition of a humanitarian?

❖ If you were given the chance to meet the person whom you consider your role model, how do you think this would change your life?

❖ Have your role models inspired you to become more Christ-like in your life?

❖ Read Hebrews 12:14 and Revelation 21:4.

CHAPTER 8
THE TEST OF A LIFETIME

I will never forget Mother Teresa's blessing.

"My dear little Laura," she said, "remember to always help others and never forget to share."

These words are golden to me and are locked in my heart. The remarkable gift of helping others by sharing with them proved itself as soon as we got home that day we met with her.

When we arrived home and unwrapped the ten-pound box of chocolate she gave us, my eyes lit up with excitement. I was not excited to eat the wonderful chocolate but rather to share this special gift.

My mother sat me down next to her and said, "Laura, what should we do with this special chocolate?"

With the happiest smile, I replied, "Mami, we have to share half of it with all our neighbors."

"What about the other half?" she asked.

"We have to share the other half with all our cousins, wherever they live," I told her.

My mother then asked the most challenging question of all. "What about yourself, Laura?"

My response was, "I'll just try a little bit. I'll be much happier if others can enjoy this chocolate. Mother Teresa set an example to always share what we have. I want to do what Mother Teresa said because I want to be like Mother Teresa."

Even at such a young age, I learned to appreciate the gift of helping others by sharing with them. My greatest passion is helping people, whether this means providing things for them or helping them through my actions. Helping others brightens my countenance and warms my heart. Mother Teresa encouraged me to always share, and this continues to be my lifelong aspiration.

Laura's Reflection on *The Test of a Lifetime*

Having the opportunity at such a young age
to receive Mother Teresa's message of sharing with
people holds great significance in my life. I feel joyful when
I share whatever I have, especially food. Sharing food
with people brings me a warm feeling of love—the happiness in people's faces is a great reward. Sharing our daily
bread makes it even more delicious for us to enjoy. I have
learned to be content with a small amount of whatever I
have because if I know I am helping others, I am fulfilled.
When I told my mother to share the chocolate Mother Teresa
gave us with other children, I knew that I would
enjoy my small piece even more, knowing others were enjoying
it as well. It taught me to never be selfish but rather to always
be generous by putting others first.

When we put others before ourselves, we exemplify unconditional love and appreciation.

Study Guide Companion

❖ If you were handed a million dollars, what would you do? Would you keep it all for yourself, or would you share the wealth with others?

❖ What effect does sharing have on you?

❖ When others share with you, how does that make you feel?

❖ Read Acts 20:35.

CHAPTER 9
GIVE AND YOU WILL RECEIVE

Since the day we were blessed by Mother Teresa, we truly believe the more you give, the more you will receive. This is especially true when one gives with love, expecting nothing in return, and that is exactly what my mother witnessed shortly after being blessed by Mother Teresa.

On a beautiful spring morning in May 1994 (I was eight years old), I asked my mother, who taught English at my school, to go to the store with me to buy a bag of cookies during our lunch break. When we entered the store, my mother saw a tall blond man, wearing a red-white-and-blue T-shirt, khaki shorts, and flip-flops, trying to communicate with the saleswoman in English, who was unable to understand a word he said.

My mother, as always, immediately stepped in to help:

"Sir, can I help you?" she said in English.

The man, smiling, replied: "Oh, yes! You speak English? Thank you very much! We are a group of Americans who have come to Durrës, Albania, for a few days on a ship called The Spirit. We stopped in Albania because we wanted to get to know Albania, the people, and the culture."

In her usual hospitable way, my mother invited them over to our house for a visit that same afternoon.

"The three people who will surely come," the man said, accepting the invitation, "are my wife, my son, and me."

After arriving home, my mother immediately began to cook joyfully.

"Fredi, dear, please go and buy a Coca-Cola for the child who is coming."

Coca-Cola was hard to find in Albania then, and my mother thought the child would want one.

My father left and bought a one-liter bottle of Coca-Cola.

Me during lunch at our house. Durrës, Albania.

When we welcomed our American guests, there were five, not just the man and his family. They had invited two more children to come with them.

They were very impressed by the royal spread my mother had prepared, especially since she did not know them and she had put it together so quickly.

During dinner, my mother poured the Coca-Cola for the children. When she saw it was running low, she realized there would not be enough for all the children to have a refill and so she sent my father to buy another bottle. My mother prayed that the Coca-Cola would not run out until my father arrived home with more. As my mother kept filling up the big glasses, we all witnessed with our own eyes that, instead of decreasing, the Coca- Cola was increasing. What would usually serve only about five glasses, served ten! The drink kept increasing to the point that we no longer needed the extra bottle.

God saw what was happening and helped my mother when she needed Him. The more my mother gave, the more she received from God. Though in the natural realm it may seem ridiculous that God would bother with such a small matter, we must remember that God cares about every little detail of our lives. He hears and answers our simplest prayers. The miraculous quite often shows up in the mundane things of life. Yes, God is in the details.

The next morning my mother witnessed another miracle. The previous night, after our American guests had left, my mother washed all the dishes with the exception of the rice pot, she had left this pot to soak overnight. To her amazement, the next morning when she opened the pot, it was completely filled with rice. My mother recalled Sister Clarisse's maxim, "The more you give, the more you will receive. God will never leave you hungry."

Just as we took care of and shared our food with our American guests, this was God's message that He was taking care of us by making our food plentiful. This gave us faith to always believe that the more you give, the more you will receive.

Laura's Reflection on *Give and You Will Receive*

The experience of inviting strangers to our house and sharing our food with them taught me that the more I give, the more I will receive. I witnessed that the more food we offered our American guests, the more food God provided for us. When you give with love, God is your witness and He will meet all your needs.

Have you ever invited people for dinner and found yourself with a lot of leftover food?

I am a firm believer that we should give with love without expecting anything in return. When you do a good deed, however, you will always be blessed in some way, and sometimes when you least expect it.

Study Guide Companion

❖ Do you believe in the expression "The more you give, the more you will receive?"

❖ Do you give with love or with the idea of expecting something in return?

❖ Read Luke 6:38 and Acts 20:35.

❖ How often do you invite people over for lunch or dinner?

❖ What effect does the gift of hospitality have on you?

❖ Read Romans 12:9–11.

❖ Do you believe in the miracle of multiplication?

❖ Read Mathew 15:32–38 and 1 Kings 17:16.

CHAPTER 10
A MIRACULOUS DREAM

Sometime after our unforgettable meeting with Mother Teresa, my mother had a miraculous dream. Describing her dream to us, and to many others later on, she recounted the following:

"I was standing on a road when I saw a big green-yellow crocodile right in front of me. I was so frightened, I called some boys and told them to kill it. In the dream, I refused to witness the killing because my heart could not bear to watch it. The boys killed the crocodile and threw it in a large deep hole, where it sank to the bottom. As the crocodile was sinking, yellow bubbles formed in the dirty, foamy water, making a loud obnoxious noise. All of a sudden, the water became crystal clear."

Continuing to narrate her dream she said:

"Standing alone next to the hole, I could see my reflection in the crystal-blue water. The water then became as clear as a mirror and a miracle happened. The face of Christ appeared in the crystal water, smiling at me."

"What did Jesus look like?" I asked.

"Jesus was wearing a white robe with a huge sparkling silver cross on His chest. When He smiled at me, I was overtaken with joy and called out to others to come see. 'Come, come everyone, it is Jesus Christ! By the time all the people came, Jesus' face had disappeared. Right at this point, I woke up."

My mother's strong connection to and belief in God was growing each day. She went from dreaming about Mother Teresa to now dreaming about Jesus Christ.

What puzzled my mother was the significance of the crocodile in the first part of her dream. And so she decided to go to the House of Missionaries of Charity and share her dream with Sister Clarisse.

My mother met with Sister Clarisse and said, "Sister Clarisse, I feel that I should tell you the dream I had last night because it will truly touch you in the core of your heart."

As my mother was explaining the dream to Sister Clarisse, her eyes filled with tears as she held tightly to my mother's hand.

"First of all, my dear Marjeta," said Sister Clarisse, "we all wish we would be so lucky as to have Jesus Christ appear in our dreams for just one second but I've never heard of Him appearing to any of us. It is a true miracle that He appeared to you. It is extremely rare that Jesus Christ appears in people's dreams, but He appeared to you because you are a person with such an enormous heart who truly has a spiritual connection with Him."

Looking at my mother intently, she ended her tribute, saying, "You will see that something very special will happen to you very soon."

My mother was thrilled to hear that something extraordinary was going to happen to her. And, indeed, it happened in a most unexpected way.

On a beautiful summer day in 1994, my mother met one of her colleagues from school for lunch. My mother mentioned to her friend how she had promised Mother Teresa that she would make it her lifelong goal to teach children from all over the world, spreading the message of sharing and forgiving and loving one another to everyone she met.

When my mother's friend heard this, she told her about an amazing opportunity.

"There is a lottery that could bring you to America where you could fulfill your dream."

My mother's colleague had read an ad in the newspaper about a lottery called the "Green Card Lottery Program." The program gave applicants a chance to come to America and become United States citizens.

"Why not give it a try? You have nothing to lose and everything to gain," my mother's friend told her.

Since very few people in Albania had heard about this lottery program, my mother decided not to discuss it with my father. She was sure he would not believe it and would advise her not to apply. Instead, my mother discussed this with my brother who encouraged her to give it a try.

Of course, my mother did not imagine she would be so lucky as to win this remarkable lottery, but she decided to take a leap of faith and give it a try. She wrote all our names and birth dates on a piece of paper and mailed them to the indicated address.

At the post office, the woman who worked there, reading the address on the envelope said, "Professor Marjeta, I hope and pray you win this lottery, because if there is anyone who deserves to win it is you. Why, you have taught all of our children English. You truly deserve to be in America."

My mother thanked her very much for her kind words and left the post office still doubtful she would win.

After a few months passed, my mother seemed to forget all about the lottery. One beautiful day in October 1994, my mother had a friend over for lunch, and while we were eating, we heard something being slipped under the front door. My mother walked over to investigate and discovered a large white envelope with a return address of Portsmouth, New Hampshire, USA.

At first glance she thought, I don't subscribe to any magazines. What could this be? As she walked back toward the kitchen, she realized it could have something to do with the lottery. She rushed in and opened it up.

She started to read it out loud:

"Dear Mrs. Marjeta Qirko, Congratulations! We are pleased to inform you that you have been the first person from Europe to ever win the Green Card Lottery Program."

As my mother continued to read the letter, she could not believe her eyes. The computer had chosen her name out of thousands of names from all over Europe, and she had won the lottery to go to her dream country, the United States of America. God was answering Mother Teresa's prayer that He lead her on a successful path for her future.

When my father arrived home from work that afternoon, my mother told him she had very exciting and almost unbelievable news to share with him.

"Without your consent, I sent our names and birth dates for the chance of a lifetime to win the lottery to come to America. Today, we found out I won this lottery and am the first person to have won it in all of Europe!"

At first my father did not believe it. In fact, he told her she was probably just imagining things, but then she proved it to him by showing him the letter, along with the documents we had to fill out. At that moment, the whole family huddled together and jumped for joy. We believed this was a sign from God that it was my mother's mission to teach children from all over the world and to spread Mother Teresa's message of sharing our daily bread and forgiving and loving one another.

We could not wait to take this journey, a journey that would change our lives forever.

Laura's Reflection on A Miraculous Dream

God's providence led us to be the first family from Europe to win the Green Card Lottery. Coming to the United States after receiving our blessing from Mother Teresa taught me that miracles often happen when you least expect them. Winning this special lottery was truly a miracle and a blessing. What was most important about winning the Green Card Lottery was that my family and I were going to legally immigrate to the United States of America by a formal invitation from the US government.

They did several background checks on my family to make sure that we were good people, entering the United States with the right motives. As my mother was an English teacher and my father was the chief of air traffic control in the Tirana Airport, both my parents were highly qualified people who could offer a lot to the United States.

The invitation to immigrate to the United States was a unique opportunity in our lives. Immigration today is a global issue. Many immigrants are coming to this country illegally. It is critical that every step of the immigration process be done in the right way. When people come to the United States in the right way, ready to give their talents to this country, we can live in a more harmonious America.

Study Guide Companion

❖ Do you know any immigrants in the United States? If so, have they come here legally or illegally?

❖ How does legal or illegal immigration change a country?

❖ If you were given the opportunity of immigrating to the country of your dreams, would you do it?

❖ In reading the above three scriptures, what does God have to say about obeying the laws of the land?

❖ Read Romans 13:1–14, Hebrews 13:17, and Romans 13:1–7.

CHAPTER 11
AN AMERICAN MISSION

On a beautifully sunny September morning in 1994, my mother was cooking a delicious meal in the kitchen. I could smell the spicy aroma of fried Albanian meatballs.

There was a knock at the door, and I thought to myself, "This knock reminds me of the knock on September 23, 1991—I wonder why?"

When my mother opened the door she saw a tall handsome man with dark-brown hair and dark-brown eyes, dressed in a formal suit. The man was accompanied by the sweetest little old lady with grey hair and a wrinkled face.

My mother said, *"Mirë mëngjes si mund t'ju ndhimojë?"* which in Albanian means "Good morning how can I help you?"

The tall man responded in a southern American accent, saying, "Madame, we are looking for Professor Marjeta Qirko. Would that be you?"

"Yes, sir, indeed that is correct. I am Marjeta Qirko."

The gentleman then kindly asked, "May we please come inside?"

"Yes, of course, please come in. Welcome to our home. How can I help you?"

The man and woman sat down. The man then said, "Good morning, Marjeta Qirko. My name is Jay Johnson and this is my mother, Elizabeth Johnson. We are from Texas in the United States and we have come to Albania on a mission. We are Jehovah's Witnesses and would

From left to right: Mr. Jay Johnson, Mrs. Barbara Johnson, and my grandmother Aleksandra eating lunch at my grandparents' house in Tirana, Albania.

like to introduce the Albanian community to our faith. In order to be successful in carrying out our mission we must learn the Albanian language.

"You were recommended by a former student of yours who is now a French teacher in Albania. She told us that if anyone is interested in learning the Albanian language well and in a short period of time, there is only one name we need to know: Marjeta Qirko. I have come to Albania with my mother Elizabeth, my wife Barbara, and our youngest daughter, Jael. We need to learn the most important words and phrases in the Albanian language. We are ready to sign a contract for six months with whatever amount of money you desire. Please tell us whether you would consider teaching us and how much you would charge us."

My mother know nothing about this man and his family, except that she wanted to help them just as she helps everyone. Overwhelmed, she told Mr. Johnson, "Please wait a minute while I discuss this with my husband." My mother called my father into the room and had a private conversation with him in Albanian.

"Fred, I don't want to charge any money because we are the same people with more or less money. Money will not buy us happiness, but doing a good deed will certainly fill our hearts with joy. I want to carry on the mission of Mother Teresa to help as much as I can. I think the best decision I can make is to do it for charity, free of charge. Mother Teresa always told us the more you give, the more you will receive."

"You are absolutely right, Marjeta. I agree with you 100 percent," my father said.

Upon receiving my father's approval, my mother turned to Jay Johnson and his mother and said, "Dear Mr. Johnson. First of all, it is such an honor to have you in my house today and I feel privileged to know that you were recommended to me by one of my best former students, for whom I have high respect. After discussing it with my husband, I have come to a decision. Even though right now life for us in Albania is not that easy, having small salaries and two children to support, I have decided to sign the contract with one condition: I do it free of charge."

Mr. Johnson was surprised indeed.

"Am I understanding you correctly, Mrs. Qirko? Are you saying you are willing to teach us however many hours we request, free of charge?"

My mother happily replied, "Yes, that is exactly right!"

"Wow! I have been a businessman for more than twenty years and have had to sign many contracts in my career, but I have never heard of signing a contract for zero amount. We appreciate your generous offer, and we will be grateful to you now and always. Thank you from the bottom of our hearts."

My mother saw this as another opportunity sent by God. She invited Mr. Johnson and his mother to stay for lunch and try her delicious Albanian meatballs. The hospitality my mother possesses is one of the characteristics inherited from her mother and father and reinforced by Mother Teresa. She was following Mother Teresa's way of sharing her daily bread with other people. Jay Johnson was shocked to meet such an incredibly generous and hospitable woman.

My mother worked very hard with the Johnson family. Not only did she teach them Albanian every day, she also had them over for lunch on a daily basis to fully immerse them in the Albanian culture. She cooked different Albanian dishes, such as *tavë me speca të mbushur* (stuffed peppers), *fasule* (traditional Albanian bean soup), *lakror* (cheese and spinach pie), and *tavë kosi* (baked lamb in yogurt). God provided plenty of food for these daily meals. My mother constantly thought about Sister Clarisse's words of wisdom: "The more you give, the more you will receive. The more food you share, the more food you will have." Therefore, we would sit down with the Johnson family and eat meals like a big, happy Albanian-American family.

During our free time we visited the Johnsons to give them more practice using the Albanian language. Both my father and my brother, who at that time was a teenager, spoke very good English. I was the only one who did not speak English—I was only nine years old. Mr. Johnson's daughter was my age so, as we played together, we were learning each other's language. During the weekends we would accompany the Johnson family to different cities, towns, and villages in Albania so they could meet the locals.

When my mother won the Green Card Lottery to come to the United States, she was excited to share the news with the Johnson family and get helpful feedback from them about the United States. Mr. Johnson encouraged my mother to do her best to become an English teacher in the United States, as well as teaching Albanian in order to help others like them learn the language. He even wrote my mother a recommendation letter for when she began applying for jobs:

"To Whom It May Concern,

In regard to Marjeta Qirko, an Albanian English teacher.

When we arrived in Albania to work here, we needed a qualified bilingual English-Albanian tutor to help us not only learn Albanian but the Albanian customs and culture as well. While looking for such a qualified person, we were referred to Mrs. Marjeta Qirko. Although we had barely begun to break the surface of this most complex language, Mrs. Qirko not only showed herself to be competent, but actually a highly qualified instructor. We are grateful to have found such a capable and articulate teacher.

As we have gotten more established here in Durrës, Albania, the question often comes up as to who our Albanian teacher is. Once we say who, we are invariably told that we have an excellent teacher. We found a doctor who speaks English. It turns out that he was one of her students . . . a good recommendation in itself. Also a great help in our learning the language is that both her husband, Fred, and her son, Dritan, speak very good English when we visit, and help us to grasp their language better.

As welcomed guests to our home in the United States, we feel that this industrious woman and her family should receive a warm welcome to our country.

Sincerely,

Jay Johnson

Having this letter from such an important American businessman meant the world to my mother. She knew that the letter would help open doors to becoming an English teacher in the United States, which was her dream. As she welcomed the mission with open arms and followed Mother Teresa's example of charity, God repaid her from the Johnson family in a different way by receiving such a beautiful thank-you letter at the end of her experience with them. God always is present and sees what good deeds people do each day and repays those good deeds when one least expects it.

Laura's Reflection on *An American Mission*

The experience of witnessing my mother teach Albanian free of charge to an American Jehovah's Witness and his family taught me that we should always be charitable without judging people based on their nationality, faith, or religion. Religious tolerance is what each person must possess in order to learn about different cultures and different people. Religious tolerance keeps one from discriminating against others who follow a different religious path. (I am not referring here to extremists.)

When my mother learned that the Johnson family were Jehovah's Witnesses, she did not judge them based on their faith. She looked at them as dear friends, not as believers of an opposing religion. She believed she would learn from them just as much as they would learn from her. My mother and my entire family welcomed them into our house and made them feel like part of the family. Despite people's religion, we must exhibit religious tolerance because we can each learn more about the diversity in this world by doing so. We must respect others, seeking to understand them without discriminating against them on the basis of their faith. Let us listen and learn more about the diverse religious world we live in.

Study Guide Companion

❖ Does knowing a person's religion affect how you treat them?

❖ Do you believe in religious tolerance? Why or why not?

❖ Do you discriminate against someone based on their religion, race, or culture?

CHAPTER 12
ANOTHER RECOMMENDATION LETTER

My mother was eager to share our miraculous news—that we were moving to the United States—with Sister Clarisse, whose prayers and blessings she cherished.

At the convent, my mother shared the following with the Sisters: "I am very happy to be here today to share another miraculous happening. A few months ago I shared a dream with Sister Clarisse and asked for her opinion as to what it meant. Sister Clarisse told me that God was planning something big for me very soon. I believed Sister Clarisse with all my heart, but I never thought a miracle such as this would happen.

"God is giving me the great opportunity to go to the country of my dreams, the United States of America. I am here to let you know that I have just won the Green Card Lottery. I was the first person in Europe the computer chose to win this lottery. Living in the United States has been a dream of mine since I was a little girl. It was this dream of one day going to America that sparked my passion for teaching the English language. I have always loved America for being a melting pot filled with immigrants from all around the world. What I am most happy about is that while teaching in America I can transmit the message of Mother Teresa of sharing our daily bread, forgiving one another, and loving and helping each other. So a wonderful future is waiting for me across the Atlantic Ocean. I am ready to conquer whatever comes my way in order to carry on my mission."

The Sisters were astonished. Their eyes filled with tears of joy and their hearts filled with love.

My mother continued, saying, "Sister Clarisse, it has been an honor to be your teacher for three years. It was the greatest pleasure coming in and being welcomed by all your beautiful smiles filled with love. You have not only been the best students of my career but you have become my dear sisters. We are one family. It breaks my heart to pieces that I will have to say goodbye to all of you, but you will always be on my mind and I will always keep you close in my heart. I am asking you a huge favor. I would be grateful if you could write a letter of recommendation for me to take to the United States."

Sister Clarisse answered and said, "Marjeta, I don't know where to start. First of all you have been an inspiration for all of us. You have showed us by your generous gestures through these three years what the real definition of a humanitarian is. You have not only been the best teacher we could have ever asked for but also our dear and beloved friend. I am so happy and proud of you because what you promised that special day to our beloved Mother Teresa you want to make a reality. God will be with you! We usually don't give recommendation letters, but we will gladly write one for you, because you deserve nothing but success and we will pray that is what you get because of your strong belief in God. We all will pray for you and your mission."

The Sisters smiled at my mother, showing the respect and love they cherished in their hearts for her.

The recommendation letter, written by Sister Clarisse and sealed with the stamp of the Missionaries of Charity, stated:

"We are writing to you this present letter to inform you that we have been students of Marjeta Qirko. She was teaching the Albanian language to all of us and the English language to those of us who did not know English, during her free time for three years. We give you all our best recommendations.

In faith, Sister Clarisse, Missionaries of Charity"

Though the letter was short in length, it was worth a thousand words.

Laura's Reflection on *Another Recommendation Letter*

The experience of my mother receiving the recommendation letter from the Sisters of Mother Teresa taught me that all hard work always pays off in one way or another. In life whatever hard work you do, you will be rewarded. Even if you are not rewarded financially, you will be rewarded in another way, perhaps by receiving appreciation for the work you have done. My mother set the example for me that when we do work with love, the appreciation we receive is precious.

To this day whenever I do something voluntarily without accepting money, receiving a thank you is a beautiful feeling. As a teacher, I write a lot of recommendation letters for my students, wherein I pour out my heart, telling about their individual good talents and hard work. And if they get accepted to their preferred university, it warms my heart when they tell me they got in. No matter what profession you are in, God, and hopefully others, will appreciate it. Appreciation is a good expression to give and receive.

Study Guide Companion

❖ What does appreciation mean to you and how do you show appreciation to others?

❖ Have you ever written a recommendation letter for someone? Has anyone written one for you? How did it made you feel?

❖ What do you appreciate most in your life?

CHAPTER 13
A TEARFUL FAREWELL

As the day of our departure for America was approaching, bitter-sweet feelings prevailed. Although we were thrilled to set out on the journey to our dream destination, we were also terribly sad to leave so many loved ones behind.

In our hometown of Durrës, my mother and father had formed loving friendships—friendships that were never going to be the same after we left Albania. For my parents, leaving for America was the toughest decision they had ever faced because they would have to say goodbye and be separated from their beloved parents and siblings. For my brother and me, it was also difficult. We had to say goodbye to our childhood friends, dear ones we had known since we were babies and whom we treasured like gold.

Not only would we be leaving behind our family and friends, but we also would be saying goodbye to the house in Durrës. After consulting with my grandparents, my parents decided to sell the house we loved so dearly. Day by day, the house became emptier as we packed up our stuff, giving away as much as we could. This was a big opportunity for my mother to demonstrate Mother Teresa's message of helping one another by sharing what we had.

My mother and me in our beloved home in Durrës, Albania, 1994.

I will never forget the day my mother opened up our house and invited our neighbors and friends to come and take whatever they pleased. Our house was filled with the most beautiful crystal, china, and silverware from around the world. My mother decided to follow Mother Teresa's

example of sharing. Instead of taking all her things to America, she decided to give her most precious and valuable possessions to people who were dear to her heart. The moment the doors of the house opened, people rushed in and took whatever they wanted. All day long, people called my mother "Nënë Teresa," which means "Mother Teresa" in Albanian, because her generosity had reached such a high level.

Me in my house in Durrës, right before coming to the United States. The fan behind me was one of the items given to my neighbors.

I remember I was so happy that day seeing the shining faces of the recipients of this largesse, hearing them thanking my mother and wishing her the brightest and most prosperous future in the United States. As the house completely emptied, it hit us that after we stepped out of the house it was never going to be ours again. From this day forward we could no longer call this house our home. We needed to focus on our hope that a better life was waiting for us in the United States.

It was heartbreaking when we said goodbye to our dear family members. My mother was very attached to her parents. She was leaving behind the people who were as dear to her as her own eyes. The moment she saw them, she could no longer keep her tears from flowing. Her eyes swelled because she could not stop the tears. Among the many words that touched her that day, the words that remain golden in her heart, are the words her beloved father whispered as he was kissing his beloved daughter goodbye: "Your children are angels, don't ever forget that!"

As my mother slowly left her parents' house, she turned around and blew them warm kisses. Though we knew we planned to return to Albania and visit our dear family very soon, it was painful parting with our loved ones and heading to a different continent an ocean away.

The Sisters of Mother Teresa came to see us off in the airport with broken hearts because their beloved teacher was leaving. As they hugged and kissed us, we somehow felt Mother Teresa's presence. Still, leaving Albania we felt as if rocks were crushing our hearts to tiny bits but we had to be brave.

We were heading in a direction that was going to change our lives forever.

From left to right: an Albanian woman, my mother, and me. We were on the plane from Rome, Italy, to Boston, United States of America. March 16, 1995.

Laura's Reflection on *A Tearful Farewell*

The experience of having to say goodbye to my family and friends, my house in Durrës, and my beloved country Albania taught me to always cherish every moment of my life. It was extremely difficult to part with people so dear to my heart since for I knew for some it could be the last time we saw each other. Knowing this, I cherished even more all the beautiful memories we had made together. Leaving our house in Durrës taught me that the best thing to do when moving from a house is to give as many of your belongings away to people who are dear to you. When you know those people are enjoying what you once enjoyed so much, it makes those items even more meaningful because it gives them a new significance. The items passed from one person to another live a much longer life.

Study Guide Companion

❖ Have you ever had to move from one house to another, from one city to another, or from one country to another? What was the experience like for you?

❖ What are some of the fondest memories you cherish with regard to a particular location?

❖ Have you ever had to give up something dear for a better life in return?

CHAPTER 14

A FOREIGN LAND

"Ready for takeoff!" The words made my heart skip a beat because I knew I had to say goodbye to my beloved mother country, Albania. As I squeezed my mother's hand, we both prayed to God to make this journey the most successful journey of all. As I placed my face against the small oval window, I saw the wonderful Albanian mountains and cliffs surrounded by the beautiful crystal blue waters of the Adriatic Sea. I had the fondest childhood memories of swimming in the Adriatic Sea from April to October. Oh, how much I would miss the taste of its salty water and the smell of the seaweed. I saw my beloved Durrës with its port in front of our house. I recalled seeing the ships every day from our balcony. Oh, how much I was going to miss waking up to the sounds of the waves of the sea and the sirens of the ships coming from all around the world.

I turned to my mother and said, "Mami, Mami, look it's our home! Goodbye, dear home, goodbye, dear Durrës, goodbye dear Albania!"

My mother responded, "Yes, Laura, this was our home and as we say goodbye to it, another home in the United States awaits us."

***

Leaving Albania was a difficult decision for my father since it meant he was going to give up his job as the chief air traffic controller at Tirana Airport. A few months before my mother won the Greencard Lottery, my father received a job offer to work in the airport of Vienna, Austria. As we were all planning to say goodbye to our life in Albania and say hello to our new life in Austria, God was making other plans for us, to bring my mother to her dream job.

Before making our decision to come to America, my father and mother discussed our two options: moving to Austria or moving to America. Because my mother had told Mother Teresa about her hope to one day teach students from all around the world in order to spread her message, my mother and father decided to move to America. Because my mother was going to pursue her dream job in America, my father was willing and ready to do any job in America that was available.

***

As the plane was picking up altitude it took my breath away to see the fluffy white clouds that looked like soft cotton pillows. I thought I was in a beautiful dream. We were all overwhelmed by the beauty we saw as the plane slowly descended. I was nine and a half years old when we arrived in Boston, Massachusetts, on March 16, 1995. As I was walking with my family through the crowded corridors of Logan International Airport, we had no idea what awaited us.

We were strangers in a foreign land, immigrants thousands of miles away from home. All I could see were strange signs and people communicating in different languages. I had heard of people immigrating to the United States, but it was different this time. I was witnessing this firsthand.

We knew very few people in Massachusetts. My mother had planned to go to Worcester since one of her friends lived there; however, things turned out differently. Chris, who had been a former English student of my mother's, greeted us in the airport and was the first person to welcome us to the United States. He lived in the city of Brockton, so the first place he took us was Brockton. He planned to drive us to Worcester the next day. But after we arrived, it was as if someone whispered to us that Brockton was the city we were destined to live in.

Upon arriving in Brockton, our friend took us to his house. He lived in a three-story house owned by two Greek ladies. The

My mother in front of our house in Brockton, Massachusetts, 1995.

women lived on the first floor; our friend lived on the second floor; and fortunately for us, the third floor was newly remodeled and ready to rent. After looking over the apartment, we fell in love with it. We decided to stay and Brockton became our hometown.

The first week in the United States was a difficult week for my family. It was an enormous transition moving from such a small country like Albania, where we knew so many people, to one of the biggest countries in the world, the United States, where we were strangers to almost everyone in our new hometown of Brockton.

My mother and me in our new home in Brockton, Massachusetts, 1995.

That week was a struggle because we tried to do things as quickly as possible. We furnished our new apartment to make it resemble our beloved home in Durrës. My parents immediately started applying for jobs, and my brother and I enrolled in school. I was enrolled in the Kennedy Elementary School, which had one of the best bilingual programs in Brockton.

For me, going to school in America was a big challenge. It was not only a culture shock, but also a linguistic challenge as I did not know how to speak English well. My mother had taught me some English before we came to the United States, but my English was not fluent. I knew only simple phrases, such as, "Thank you!" "Goodbye" "How are you?" "My name is..." I started third grade the second week in the country and was placed in a bilingual program. The school told us I would probably stay in that program until the end of that school year and possibly for the following school year as well.

I will never forget that first week of school. I was still a child, one who had not much of an idea how to communicate with these foreign people. I felt as if I was completely lost. The language barrier made me feel like an outsider who did not belong.

The American culture seemed to be completely different from my Albanian background. It surprised me that American children often took field trips to Boston or Plymouth to learn about the history of their country. And the idea of a thirty-minute lunch followed by recess was so strange to me. In Albania I was used to going to school from eight o'clock in the morning until noon when all the children went home to eat lunch. Then, after one o'clock, all the children went back to school for a couple of hours. The first week, staying in school for eight hours in a row on a daily basis, seemed strange. It was also hard because I felt so isolated. I did not know anyone and, as friendly as I was by nature, it was not easy to make friends because I could not communicate with them.

Laura's Reflection on *A Foreign Land*

The experience of being an immigrant in a foreign country taught me that you must work very hard to succeed in a foreign land. When you are given the opportunity to immigrate to a country like America, you must take full advantage and try to succeed in every way possible. You must start by finding a home, finding a job, finding a school, finding new friends, in other words, finding a new way of life. If you can't find a job in your profession like the one you had back in your country, don't let that discourage you. Be open-minded and welcome any job (that's legal of course) will bring in money for you and your family. If you have the courage and the patience to work hard to earn the job of your dreams, like my mother did, then let nothing stop you and go for it—even if it means that you must go to the university again or take graduate courses for your degree from your country to be recognized in America.

All immigrants coming to the United States face this difficult challenge of not necessarily finding jobs in their chosen professions if their degrees from back home are not recognized in America. I encourage those immigrants to push themselves hard and let nothing stand in the way of making their dreams a reality in this great land of opportunity. If you are a student like my brother and I were, take full advantage of your education and study hard, for your hard work will pay off later in life. Don't let any obstacles stand in your way; always be optimistic. For me, learning English as an immigrant was a great obstacle, but with patience and determination I overcame that obstacle very quickly. We must always try to face challenges and persevere if we want to live successful lives in America or anywhere else in the world.

With hard work take advantage of the opportunities that are presented to you and make your dreams come true.

Study Guide Companion

❖ What has been the greatest obstacle in your life? Were you able to overcome it?

❖ Imagine if you were an immigrant in a foreign land, how would you feel? What would you do?

❖ How hard would you work to make your dreams become a reality?

CHAPTER 15

A PASSION FOR LEARNING

As a girl from Albania, learning English was one of the most difficult challenges

I have ever had to face. Sometimes I thought I would never be able to learn this complex language. However, I am an optimistic person, a person who constantly strives to do her best.

Me when I attended the Kennedy School in Brockton, Massachusetts, in 1995.

I set a goal to learn English as quickly as possible, not only to communicate but also as a way to start making new friends. In class I would try to participate in class discussion as much as possible even though I knew I was making grammatical mistakes. My theory was that the more mistakes I made, the more I would learn. That proved to be correct. I recall applying this theory every day as I practiced using the language with my favorite teacher, Mrs. Lorraine Luisi. She pushed me so hard and encouraged me to reach for the stars. Because of the mistakes I made and my positive motivation, I was picking up English extremely quickly. As soon as I got home from school, I started doing my homework.

After finishing my homework, I would watch television, not to entertain myself but to accomplish my goal of learning English. Even today, as a foreign language teacher, I think that the best way to fully comprehend a language and learn the idioms of the language is by constantly hearing it and practicing it. I would watch shows such as "Full House", "The Price Is Right", and "Wheel of Fortune". These three shows helped me learn English within a month. When I watched "Full House", I would repeat every word each character said. I knew every single word of each episode by heart. "The Price Is Right" and "Wheel of Fortune" were the most beneficial because I mastered all the letters in the English alphabet, all the numbers, and increased my English vocabulary every day.

I talked in English until I became really good at it. My teachers were surprised and proud of my incredible progress. After two months, I was taken out of the bilingual program and placed in mainstream English classes.

My teachers met with my mother and told her about my academic progress. They advised her to place me in the fifth grade instead of the third grade because of my academic ability in subjects like math and reading. Since I would be the youngest in my class, my mother decided to turn down the offer in order to give me the opportunity to be with children my own age.

I fell in love with school and was determined to succeed. English went from what was once my greatest challenge to my biggest passion. It was this passion that helped me decide that learning and teaching foreign languages was to be my vocation. Today I hold a degree in foreign languages because I was so fortunate to come to the United States and learn English as a second language. I always attribute this to God blessing me and Mother Teresa's special prayer over me.

Laura's Reflection on *A Passion for Learning*

The experience of learning English as a second language in America as an immigrant child taught me to never fear anything that seems impossible because if you work hard for what you want, you can turn the impossible into the possible. For me learning the English language seemed impossible at first, but with determination I learned English extremely quickly. You must always push yourself to work hard to achieve success in whatever you want to achieve in life.

I also was self-motivated to learn English as a way of fitting in with the American children and making new friends. This motivated me day to day to learn the language even more quickly. At first the students made fun of me as an immigrant girl from Albania with no English communication skill. This made me even more determined to show them who I really was and to prove to them that I could do whatever they could. I wanted to teach the American children in my school that we should not make immigrants feel inferior to us, rather we should make them equal to us because they are unique just like everyone else. An immigrant is special because that person has so much more culture awareness since they have lived in another country. That person is bilingual or multilingual. We should embrace this and view immigrants as role models to follow, inspiring us to learn different languages and, when possible, travel to experience different cultures. Immigrants make this world a more diverse and colorful world to live in.

Study Guide Companion

❖ Have you ever discriminated or know someone who has discriminated against an immigrant? How did it make him or her feel?

❖ Would you consider yourself superior or inferior to an immigrant? Why or why not?

❖ Have you ever overcome an obstacle that seemed impossible to overcome? How has this affected or changed you?

CHAPTER 16

A CHERISHED CHRISTMAS CARD

Even though we moved an ocean away from our beloved Albania, we always had our dear Sisters of Mother Teresa on our minds. My mother was spiritually connected with the Sisters through prayer every day. She loved to meditate on what Mother Teresa taught us about prayer: "Prayer is not asking. Prayer is putting oneself in the hands of God, at His disposal, and listening to His voice in the depth of our hearts."

My mother wanted to send Sister Clarisse and all the other Sisters this message; therefore, before Christmas my mother decided to write to Sister Clarisse a beautiful card and letter with the following version of the message.

Dear Sister Clarisse,

There is not a day that passes by that I don't think of you and pray for you. I place myself in the hands of God and listen to His voice speaking to my heart as I thank Him for all the blessings He has bestowed upon me, you being one of them. You are in my thoughts every moment in every way.

Since we have relocated to the United States, it has been your prayers and God's will that has made our move to the United States as successful as it has become. We have created a beautiful home here in Brockton, Massachusetts; a home that, just like our home in Durrës, is filled with love and hospitality.

I welcome people by hosting lunches and dinners every Sunday to spread Mother Teresa's message of sharing our daily bread. I want to instill this in the minds of Laura and Dritan.

Speaking of Laura and Dritan, they are both progressing so much with the English language and assimilating quite well in the American culture. Dritan is currently in high school and has gotten his driver's license and is driving us all over the United States. Laura is attending an elementary school with exceptional grades in all of her classes. Frederik has started working very hard here in the United States just like he worked hard in Albania, and most importantly, thanks to your beautiful blessed recommendation letter, I have started working as a substitute teacher in Brockton High School, one of the largest and most diverse schools in the United States.

Thanks to all your constant prayers and blessings we are beginning a bright and prosperous future. We miss you a lot but you are constantly with us every moment and everywhere in our minds and hearts. We love you very much. May you have a blessed Holiday Season. Merry Christmas and a happy, healthy, and prosperous New Year. May God bless you!

All our love,
Marjeta, Frederik, Dritan and Laura

On a cold January night as we were warming up in front of the fireplace, an envelope was slipped underneath the door. We were surprised to see from the return address that it was from Varna, Bulgaria. We were puzzled as to who this letter could be from. Upon opening the card, we saw a card with a beautiful scene of the three wise kings bringing presents to baby Jesus.

"May the Spirit of Christmas Bring You Peace and Happiness!"

My mother read the rest of the message aloud to us:

My dearest Marjeta, family and Dritan,

Hello, How are you all? I thank you from my heart for the beautiful card and letter. I remember you and pray for you and I love you all. Jesus loves you. How much? So much. He was born and died for me and you on the cross. Prayer is the best gift from you to me. Because prayer gives new heart and mind and new life and prayer changes all things. So pray always and pray for me too. Here we had beautiful experiences.

We translated songs from English to Bulgarian. We went to sing in the hospital, Children's home, and for the old people. It was beautiful but I missed Albania. So hope to see you soon. My greetings to all.

Love and Prayers,
Sr. M. Clarisse

My mother started weeping as she said: "Wow, how extremely powerful this message is, especially since Sister Clarisse asked me to pray for her too. We know that prayer is the best gift we can give to one another and that prayer will change everything. The power of prayer made our dreams of coming to the United States a reality. It is our daily prayers to our beloved Lord that will brighten our future in this foreign land."

Laura's Reflection on *A Cherished Christmas Card*

The experience of receiving a cherished Christmas card filled with blessings from Sister Clarisse taught me to always be thankful and to always pray to God for everything. Just as Sister Clarisse said in her card to always pray to God, I have tried to always follow her saying. As she said, there is no greater gift we can give one another than prayer. We should always pray to God with great faith, for He will answer our prayers. My family prayed to God to make our transition from Albania to America smooth, and He did just that in an extraordinary way. People pray to God for many different reasons. And when the answer is no, the joy we hoped to gain through whatever we wanted on earth, we believe He will give us in heaven.

Study Guide Companion

❖ Have you ever received a letter, card, or another type message that you cherished?

❖ Do you believe that prayer is the best gift we can give to one another?

❖ How often do you pray to God?

CHAPTER 17

THE IDEAL JOB

When I was a teenager, I got to see my mother's dream of being a teacher here become a reality. And this made a deep impression on me. One day I would be teaching in the very same school!

The moment my mother found that she could move to the United States, her dream was to become an English teacher in order to carry out her life mission of sharing Mother Teresa's message. When we first came to the States, however, my mother was willing to do whatever kind of job was open to her in order to create better conditions for our family.

As my father, too, was willing to take any job, he began working as a manager of a carwash right next to our house. Though it was not his ideal job, he was very content to make money to support the family.

My mother applied to many different places for many kinds of jobs; however, surprisingly, no one called her back for an interview. Though at first it seemed strange, she came to understand that God wanted her to carry out her mission by securing a teaching position. God encouraged her, and she finally applied for a teacher position, even though she knew that it would be difficult for her as an immigrant.

To achieve this goal and retain a teaching position, my mother had to go back to Albania to get all her original transcripts and diplomas as an English teacher from the University of Tirana. This was her first trip back to Albania after five months in the United States. She thought that if she wanted things to turn out well, the first place she should go would be the House of Missionaries of Charity in Durrës to receive a blessing from the Sisters.

The day my mother paid a surprise visit to the Sisters of Mother Teresa was so emotional. Without informing any of the Sisters that she was in Albania, she showed up at the front gate of the House of Missionaries of Charity and rang the doorbell. The Sisters' screams of joy were the next sounds.

My mother and Sister Clarisse in the House of Missionaries of Charity in Durrës, during my mother's first return trip to Albania, 1995.

They greeted her full of affection: "Teacher Marjeta, teacher Marjeta, you are here, we can't believe our eyes!"

My mother remembered responding:

"My dear Sisters, I have missed you so much in these past months since I left Albania. We have been thousands of kilometers away, but we have always been spiritually connected since you have always remained in my heart and mind. You have been in my prayers every day, and I know I have been in your prayers as well. I am confident when I say this because things have gone perfectly for my family since the first day we moved to the United States.

"God is helping me and directing me in the right path that I have to follow. God is giving me courage to begin a new, prosperous life. It is because of all of you, my dear Sisters, that I have had the opportunity of becoming an English teacher in the United States, just like I had dreamed of and promised Mother Teresa to spread her message to people from all around the world, because of your beautiful recommendation letter for me.

"I am here in Albania for only one week, just to get my official documents from the University of Tirana. I felt in my heart that by coming to visit my most special and dear friends, my entire journey here in Albania would be blessed."

The Sisters huddled around my mother, surrounding her with prayers. Among the many prayers was this: "Dear Lord, please open the doors of success for the career of dear Mrs. Marjeta Qirko."

When my mother had to leave, the Sisters went to the airport to see her off. Her eyes and theirs were filled with tears of hope that soon she was going to be an English teacher in the United States and spread Mother Teresa's message to the world.

One year later, in the summer of 1996, my mother returned again to Albania, but this time with my brother and me. Of course, one of the first places we went to visit was the House of Missionaries of Charity in Durrës. When we arrived there, we were welcomed by a surprised and happy Sister Clarisse. For Sister Clarisse it was very emotional to see my brother and me again after one year of being so far away in America. She would not stop hugging and kissing us and showering us with love.

My brother, Dritan, and me with Sister Clarisse in the House of Missionaries of Charity in Durrës, during our visit to Albania, 1996.

She questioned us about how we were doing in our new country of America. She was very surprised about my rapid advancement in the English language and with my brother's growth as a young man. She advised my brother, who was so dear to her heart, to always pray to God, to always go to church, and to continue helping others just as he had done in Albania. My brother promised Sister Clarisse that he would always do that and he has kept his promise until this day.

After my mother returned to the United States, during the summer of 1995, with the Sisters' blessings, she successfully fulfilled the requirements for a teacher position. She began teaching English as a second language at Brockton High School. This academy consisted of more than four thousand students from different countries of the world.

My mother teaching her ESL students at Brockton High School, 1999.

This was not an easy job as she had to teach quite a diverse group of students, students from many different backgrounds. But in her heart she felt this was the opportunity God had given her to be in contact with students from all over the world, just as the Sisters she had taught from all around the world. She realized how important it was going to be for her not only to teach the students the English language but to also teach them the important values in life.

Teaching the English language to students at Brockton High School, she shared her knowledge about the importance of school and the family. Helping, sharing, forgiving, and respecting one another were the main components she felt the students had to fully understand.

Her focus was on teaching forgiveness, one of Mother Teresa's main messages. Equipped with forgiveness they would be able to feel a part of the "family" in such a big school. These teenagers, like most youths, often argued or fought with one another. My mother would tell them that instead of entering into conflict, to try to talk it out and come to a peaceful agreement, or to simply forgive each other for what the other might have done.

She encouraged even her weakest students that if they worked hard enough, they could achieve even what they thought would be impossible. In this method, she was just like Mother Teresa, a mother figure to the children.

My mother gave her students encouraging examples, such as: "In the future, I will be so honored to walk into a bank and find my student as the CEO, to walk into a hospital and find my student as a doctor, to walk into a court and find my student as an attorney."

She told her students to have faith, even when it seems impossible, because faith is where their strengths would lie. Even though for bilingual students who have just immigrated to this country, the idea of becoming someone important seemed like an impossible dream, my mother helped them see that impossible dreams indeed come true when a person really believes in them. Just as it is written in the gospel of Matthew: "With man this is impossible, but with God all things are possible."

My mother had used this method since beginning her teaching career in Albania, and now she would tell these stories to her American students of English as a second language.

"When I was teaching in the high school of foreign languages in Tirana, Albania, among other students, I had a student from northern Albania who didn't have a good educational background because of the difficult conditions in northern Albania. I encouraged him by giving him a better grade than he deserved, while telling him that in the future, he will be one of the best students in the school through my help. Just as I predicted, he graduated with the best results. I was so happy to see him succeed academically that I told him that in the future he would be a very important person. Years later, he became a foreign ambassador!

"Another example I recall is from Brockton High School. One of my students from Cape Verde, an island in the Atlantic Ocean off the coast of Africa, didn't speak English. He was disappointed and frustrated and he did not behave properly in class. I remembered the student I had encouraged years ago in Albania and thought to myself that I would use the same method with this student. I encouraged my Cape Verdean student by constantly helping him and by giving him a better grade than he deserved. I also told him that in the future he would be a lawyer and probably would work in the governor's office. Many years passed. When an award ceremony was held at Brockton High School for a guest of honor, guess who the guest of honor was? My Cape Verdean student! Upon entering the auditorium filled with more thank 450 people, he walked straight to me and said: "Does everyone see this woman? Mrs. Qirko is the woman I dedicate my award to because she saved my life. I started from zero, she has turned me into a hero. I am who I am today thanks to this wonderful woman."

Since a lot of the students came from very low income families, my mother would always buy presents for them whether it was chocolates or food, school materials and necessities, or even clothes. She considered her students not just as her students but as her own children because we are all the children of God. She showed no partiality between races, nationalities, skin color, and social status.

To my mother her students were all her beloved children, and her goal was to help them academically and personally as much as she could. My mother's theory was that she had to be a leader for her students and show them that if she helped one person, then that person will help another person, and so we can have a much different world. My mother each and every day showed her students the meaning of love.

My mother with one of her favorite students Chloe, who used to call her "Mama Qirko," at the Brockton High School senior prom, 2009.

Mother Teresa taught my mother that even the rich hunger for love. My mother showed her students they were cared for, that their talents were wanted and needed. Since many of them were immigrants without parents present to show them unconditional love, she became like a mother to them, and they often called her "Mother."

For seven years during the day my mother was an ESL teacher at Brockton High School and at night an ESL teacher in the Adult Learning Center in Brockton. My mother had the opportunity to work with immigrants who had just arrived in this country in pursuit of a better future, just as she had a few years before them. My mother could connect with these men and women because she understood their struggles, their concerns, and their fears as foreigners in a new country. She not only helped them learn English, but she provided emotional support as well. My mother encouraged them to learn English to the best of their ability and to pursue their dream careers in this foreign country just as she had. She was a living role model for them. All her adult students loved her and looked up to her as the inspiring person they all yearned to become.

My mother and me with her students from the Adult Learning Center in Brockton, 1999.

During her fifteen years' teaching career in the United States, my mother made a huge impact on each of her students' lives. Even to this day, no matter where she goes, if one of her students sees her, he or she stops and gives her the warmest hug and says: "Mrs. Qirko, I miss you; I miss your values; I miss your generosity; I miss your love. I am who I am today thanks to you!"

Another student said: "Mrs. Qirko. I left my mother in Cape Verde but you have become my mother. You are such a caring and helpful woman. You have treated me as if I were your child by always buying chocolates and even presents for me. I look up to you, respect you, and love you like my second mother. I always knew there were angels in the sky but in fact I found my angel in the earth by finding you!"

Hearing words like these brings the greatest pleasure. My mother's heart fills with happiness when she sees her students succeed in life and have such wonderful futures. She feels that since she was blessed by Mother Teresa and spread her message through actions, her students will also have success follow them in every path of life.

One of the most inspirational women in Brockton, Georgia Tasho, was my mother's greatest help in pursuing her teaching career. Georgia was an Albanian immigrant, just as we were. She had immigrated with her mother and father and younger sister from Korça, Albania, when she was about four years old. As an immigrant, she understood the struggles my mother faced in the process of becoming a teacher, since she, too, had been a teacher in Brockton.

My mother with Georgia Tasho in her beach cottage in Rockland, Maine.

Georgia helped my mother get connected with the right people, who led her to the right locations, who wrote letters of recommendation for her, and who helped make her dream of being an English teacher in the United States a reality. Georgia Tasho reminded my mother of Mother Teresa because she, too, had a heart filled with unconditional love for people, especially for immigrants from her beloved Albania. Georgia became like a member of our family. She is like my American Albanian grandmother. We love and cherish her very much.

Laura's Reflection on *The Ideal Job*

Witnessing my mother pursue her dream job in a foreign country taught me that when we put our minds to something we are passionate about, anything is possible. It taught me to always try to achieve my goals and make all my dreams into reality. With hard work and dedication, the sky is the limit. Even if we think the odds are totally against us, in many situations we can become whatever we want to become. My mother as a teacher served as my role model. She taught me how to take care of, respect, protect, and love my students as if they were my own children. She taught me to teach life lessons and values to them. Most importantly she taught me to always encourage my students that they can be successful. They are the generation we hope will brighten our future. No matter what work we do, we should always encourage one another. Chronic criticism of others is not helpful.

Our greatest success in life lies in the success we help make possible for others. When we see others succeed, we should always be proud, not jealous. We should always praise them, not try to bring them down. Most importantly we should always love them for the good that they manifest, not hate them for being better than or different from us. If we can achieve this, we will all live in a much happier world.

Study Guide Companion

❖ Do you believe that sometimes your success in life is linked to the success you have made possible for others?

❖ When you see a successful person, do you see that person as your role model whom you look up to or as your competitor whom you are trying to challenge?

❖ How often do you look for opportunities to encourage others?

CHAPTER 18

POEMS OF LOVE

Being blessed with a golden mother like Marjeta, it is no surprise that my mother is and has always been my greatest inspiration because she has taught me the best values in life. She is my definition of unconditional love. The love I possess for my mother is a love that is indescribable.

During my teenage years, a new passion of mine blossomed: the passion of poetry. I wrote these poems dedicated to my mother to show her that I had fully comprehended that she was my greatest inspiration in life and she was my hero. I wanted to become like her and follow in her footsteps. I wanted to follow in her footsteps just as she had followed in Mother Teresa's footsteps.

Among the many poems that I wrote, two fit perfectly in this chapter:

My Hero

Someone who loves whatever she does,
a person with a heart filled with love.
She's the greatest woman in whatever she does,
this lovely lady is my dear mom.

She loves to help people in every way,
she's trying to help them every day.
She loves to wish upon everyone happiness and love,
she's got a blessing from up above.

She's taught the Sisters of Mother Teresa three years free of charge,

and got blessings from Mother Teresa straight from her heart.

When they met, she blessed my entire family along with me,

it was an incredibly beautiful thing to see.

My mom has encouraged me to do good things,

to be outstanding in everything.

Now I understand what she is trying to do for me and so I see,

that this really amazing mother is a hero to me.

Remember My Words

Oh daughter, my dear daughter,

you must listen to what I say.

My sayings will lead you to a good way.

I know what's right for you, always,

  all the time.

I've seen your happy moments

*My mother and I in the year
I wrote my poems for her.*

  and tears when you cry.

I know what's wrong and right for you to do,

because I have been your age too.

You should never trust anyone but me.

When you become my age, darling, you will see,

There are people we love and enemies out there,

watch out for the bad ones, but don't you fear.

You'll learn to love and trust as the years go by,

you'll learn the meaning of a mother's love.

The person who is proud of everything you do,

is the person who is teaching everything to you.

You know that your mother thinks of you every day.

When you need help she's the person who will pray.

The values I have taught you, you'll always keep with you.

That's how I know you are remembering me too.

Laura's Reflection on *Poems of Love*

Writing poems of love for my mother as a teenager made me love and cherish my mother even more. It helped me understand that there is no one in this world who loves in the same way a mother loves you.

Created to carry a baby in her womb, the mother's bond with her child is different from the bond with others in the family. Mothers are sacrificial when it comes to their children. There is an old saying, "One mother can take care of one hundred children but one hundred children cannot take care of one mother." The love and devotion a devoted mother gives to a child is irreplaceable. A good mother teaches you right and wrong and is proud to see the person you become in life. In many cases a child is a reflection of his or her mother. I believe I am the woman I am today because of the way my mother raised me, the love she showed me, and the values she taught me. I am a reflection of my mother, and in the future I want my children to be a reflection of me. I believe there is no stronger and more beautiful bond than that of a mother and child. My mother is my number one—my greatest love.

Study Guide Companion

❖ 1. How would you describe your bond with your mother?

❖ 2. Who are the people you bond with the most?

❖ 3. Can you recall a time when your mother demonstrated sacrificial love in your life? How did that demonstration inspire you?

CHAPTER 19

HELPING THE REFUGEES

Since saying goodbye to Albania, our beloved mother country, we have remained spiritually connected with Albania and the Albanian community. The member of our family who is the most patriotic is definitely my brother, Dritan. Since our move to the United States, he has made it his mission to return to Albania each year to visit his friends and relatives and to help them in any way possible. He was gifted with the desire to care and share by working with the Missionaries of Charity and with the priests in Durrës. He loved helping anyone and everyone, but Albanians touched his heart the most.

Between the years 1995 and 1997, Albania was going through a devastating civil war. Every day as my brother watched the news, his heart ached for the poor refugees who were fleeing the country in hopes of a better future in countries such as Italy and Greece. My brother often mentioned how he hoped that one day he would have the opportunity to help poor refuges coming out of that war. Little did he know that soon his wish would come true.

One day my brother rushed inside the house and said to my mother: "Mom, open the refrigerator and make a huge basket of all the food we can spare. There are several refugees from Kosovo who have arrived in Brockton and need our help."

My brother had been contacted by Catholic Charities in Brockton about these people from our country. He was called to interpret for them, just as he had interpreted for the Sisters of Mother Teresa and groups of priests from the Missionaries of Charity in Albania.

Hearing my brother's request, my mother did exactly as he asked. She filled up a huge basket of food, and that night we went to the apartment complex where the refugees had been placed. We brought clothing for them as well and other necessities. On a daily basis we helped them assimilate into the United States.

My mother, my brother, and myself served as interpreters for the refugees. My mother would accompany them to places such as hospitals, stores, and the immigration office. We did this with the greatest pleasure, free of charge, following in my mother's footsteps of teaching the Sisters of Mother Teresa free of charge.

My brother, Dritan, with the Albanian flag shirt, my grandmother Aleksandra with the black dress, myself next to her with the refugees from Kosovo in our backyard for lunch.

As a family we decided that every week we would go food shopping for the refugees from Kosovo to lighten their burden of spending money on food. We would take them shopping with our own money, following the message of Mother Teresa to help people in every way we could, expecting nothing in return. We kept on this mission for years and years and were happy to have done it. We would certainly do it again if need be. We were not trying to do great things but "small things with great love," as Mother Teresa always taught. We know that good works are links that form a chain of love. When we have love, we have everything we could ever want.

Laura's Reflection on *Helping the Refugees*

The experience of helping the refugees from Kosovo taught me that there is nothing better than doing charity for the people who need it the most. It taught me that we should always help our brothers and sisters whenever they are in need. We should always open our doors and welcome people of need inside and treat them like family. We should always provide food for the needy. Immigrants touch our hearts most because we, too, were once immigrants and can fully understand their struggles. When we help immigrants it is not the quantity we give that makes an impression on them, it is the quality of our humanitarian gesture that leaves an imprint in their hearts.

By helping immigrants we are helping nations.

By helping nations we are helping the world.

By helping the world we are helping God.

Study Guide Companion

❖ 1. Have you ever helped someone in need? If so, how has that experience changed your life?

❖ 2. How does your conception of the world change when you witness charity?

❖ 3. We are not always able to do great things, but can you recall a time you did small things with great love?

CHAPTER 20

PROTECTION FROM ABOVE

Do you believe in protection from above? We surely believe this since the day we were blessed by Mother Teresa.

One morning in August 2001, my mother woke up terrified and shaking and told us about a dream she had:

"I was standing in the middle of a city next to a big river that seemed like the sea with two tall buildings near the riverbank. It was a calm, sunny day when all of a sudden out of nowhere there was a huge explosion filled with fire everywhere. The two tall buildings started to collapse. There was chaos everywhere. I started to call your name, 'Laura, Laura,' and I found you, but when I called your brother and your father, I could not find them anywhere."

My mother was so puzzled and worried about what this dream meant. A few days after this dream, my brother and my father went back to Albania for a three-week visit to family and friends. They were going to arrive back in Boston on September 11. The night of September 10, my mother and I could not sleep at all. As we tossed and turned, we of course thought this was due to the excitement of welcoming my father and my brother at the airport in Boston the next day. We planned to arrive at the airport around noon.

At around 9:00 a.m. that September 11 morning, as my mother and I were sitting in our classroom in Brockton High School, we were hit with the devastating news that two planes had crashed into the twin towers of the World Trade Center in New York City; a third plane had hit the Pentagon in Washington DC; and that a fourth plane had crashed in a field in Pennsylvania. On hearing this horrific news, we panicked! All we could think of was that my father and brother were at that moment flying into the United States. As we kept hearing the news that airports would be shutting down and that missiles might be hitting planes, we were frightened about the safety of our beloved family members.

Upon finding out about the emergency, my mother and I left the school and rushed home to call my uncle, who was the State Secretary of Albania, to ask if he knew anything about the plane my brother and father were passengers on.

My uncle replied: "The last thing I knew was that they were on the plane from Zurich, Switzerland, to Boston, Massachusetts." At this point, my father's and brother's lives were in God's hands. All we could think of was how terrified they must be and pray to God that they would come home safely.

We later learned that when they were in the air flying from Zurich to Boston and making their descent into Boston, they were informed of the tragedy and diverted to Nova Scotia, Canada. They had no way of communicating with us, and my mother and I were extremely scared.

My mother recalled her horrific dream and linked it with this event. Everything now made sense to her. Just like in my mother's dream when she saw an explosion of two tall buildings by a river (which were the twin towers in New York City by the Hudson River), and when she searched for her family members she found me (since I was currently with her on September 11), but she did not find my father and my brother just as they were nowhere to be found on September 11.

They finally came back home after spending three days in Nova Scotia. We truly believe that my mother's prayers for protection over my father and brother were answered. God was protecting them and us from above while hearing our constant prayers.

***

Here is another instance of supernatural protection. In July 2005 my family and I were on a European trip. The trip started in what has always been one of our favorite European cities, London. That year we were staying at a brand-new hotel in London's financial district. Both nights we spent there we were evacuated at 1:00 a.m. for what we thought was a fire alarm.

The morning of July 6 was a day filled with sightseeing all around London, including Buckingham Palace, Piccadilly Circus, and Trafalgar Square. At Trafalgar Square my mother's eyes caught two men whom she had a strong feeling were planning something dangerous. She immediately warned me in Albanian to leave as quickly as possible. We jumped on the last metro train and went back to the hotel. Little did we know that the next metro train leaving from the same station was going to be blown up on July 7 when a massive terror attack overtook the city. We were saved from this dreadful attack by just one day.

Even though we were in London on that day of terror, God protected us by keeping us away from the locations we had just visited the previous day. If we had waited one more day to do all our sightseeing, we might not be alive today. We were at the right place at the right time and thanks to my mother's strong intuition we avoided being at the wrong place at the wrong time. After we left London we were told we had been evacuated from the hotel two nights in a row not because of the threat of fire but because of the threat of a terror attack. It was that specific hotel that was targeted but thankfully salvaged. God sent us His protection from above.

***

My mother's strong intuition, due to constant prayer to God, saved our lives once again. This time we were flying out of London's Heathrow Airport to Boston's Logan Airport with United Airlines. As we boarded the plane, I sat in the window seat, my mother sat in the middle seat next to me, and a young American woman sat in the aisle seat next to my mother. My father and brother sat in the seats behind us.

The plane taxied down the runway. It made a final stop before takeoff. My mother was praying to God, as she always does before takeoff. Suddenly she grabbed my hand extremely tightly and I panicked. I could tell this was not a normal affectionate grab. I knew something was wrong.

In English my mother said loudly: "Stop! The plane cannot take off! There is something wrong with the engine."

Everyone turned their heads and looked at my mother as if she was crazy.

A minute after my mother's warning, a stewardess who had overheard my mother rushed to the cockpit. Immediately following this, the pilot came on the loudspeaker: "Good afternoon ladies and gentleman. This is your captain speaking. I am sorry to inform you that we cannot take off due to a serious mechanical problem in one of the plane's engines. We are lucky to have caught this problem now and apologize for the inconvenience. We will be turning the plane back to the gate, and give you more information as technicians work on fixing the engine. We thank you for your understanding and for your patience. We hope to get you up in the air back to Boston as soon as possible."

We turned back at the gate and were delayed three hours before taking off again. My mother believed that God whispered in her ears in order to save all the people in the plane. The people were astonished and could not stop looking at my mother with gratitude. Again, God spoke to my mother; he was protecting our family from above.

Another miracle occurred in 2007. That May, Brockton experienced a terrible rain storm. The entire city was under flood watch. The rain poured and the entire neighborhood flooded to the point where canoe boats were transferring people to shelters. The neighborhood reminded me of Venice with its gondolas traveling through the canals. My mother prayed that God would spare our house from the flood. To our amazement, our house remained like an island, with water all around it but without any water in our yard or inside our house.

Our house two days after the flood.

My mother's prayer was: "Jesus, please protect my house and my family from this devastating flood. Jesus I pray to you with all my heart.

Please save us, amen."

We believe my mother's strong spiritual connection with God through prayer played a role in God's protection over us.

Laura's Reflection on *Protection from Above*

Experiencing God's protection during many dangerous events taught me to fully believe in God's protection from above. If we believe in God and constantly pray, asking Him to take care of us, protect us, and save us from danger, that is exactly what He will do, certainly in eternity.

God will make sure you are in the right place at the right time. Even if you are in the wrong place at the wrong time and ask Him to save you, He will hear your prayer and do just that. If we believe in God and connect with Him through prayer, God will warn us of danger.

Have you ever felt yourself in danger and prayed to God and then felt as if He answered your prayers? God is always available when we need Him, we simply have to pray. God protects us from harm every single day.

We should never fear because God is always near.

Study Guide Companion

❖ 1. Do you believe in protection from above?

❖ 2. Have you ever been saved from danger?
   How has this changed your life?

❖ 3. Do you believe God is our Savior?

CHAPTER 21

LOVE OF LANGUAGES BREAKS RECORDS

Throughout my academic career in the United States, I have been very blessed. I have excelled throughout my elementary and secondary education and was destined to do the same in my college academic career.

One of the most exciting periods of my life was when I was choosing a college to attend. Since moving to the United States, I had fallen in love with one school: Stonehill College. I chose Stonehill College because it was a Catholic college, founded by the Congregation of the Holy Cross in Easton, Massachusetts.

What better topic could there have been for my application essay than the unforgettable experience of meeting and being blessed by Mother Teresa? As my essay was read at Stonehill, several professors and administrators encouraged me to not only publish the essay but also suggested that I consider writing a book about my personal experience and spiritual connection with Mother Teresa. I thank all my dear professors from Stonehill College for providing the first inspiration to write Touched by a Saint.

Since I was a child, I have been fortunate to have traveled all around the world. In Albania my family had the opportunity to travel thanks to my father's job as the chief of air traffic control in Tirana Airport. In America my family had the opportunity to travel thanks to my mother's job as a teacher traveling the world with students through EF Educational

Student Tours. I have traveled to more than fifty countries throughout my life and am planning to travel to many more.

Left: My mother and me in front of the Eiffel Tower in Paris, France.

Below: Me in front of Buckingham Palace in London, England.

Foreign languages have become my great love and passion. In every country I have traveled to since I was a child, I have tried to learn and remember as much of the language as possible. When choosing a major at Stonehill College, there was no doubt in my mind that foreign languages were to be my major. I selected three languages: Spanish, French, and Italian. Even though I was a triple major and a philosophy minor, which required long hours of difficult work, I excelled in my studies because I loved what I was studying. People were astonished that with such a load I was consistently an A student. My love of languages drove me to achieve excellence.

Foreign language majors are required to study abroad. I was thrilled about this opportunity, but because I was determined to graduate in three years, I wanted to push myself harder and do something different. Under-graduate students usually study abroad during either the fall or the spring semester. I didn't want to take up an entire semester, so instead, I decided to study abroad in the summer. I knew this decision was going to be difficult since studying abroad in the summer would mean more intensive work in less time.

After reflecting several days about my desire to be accepted into this program, I became even more determined that this is what I wanted to achieve. I asked to talk to the department chair of foreign languages, Dr. Martinez, about my decision.

"Laura, I know you are full of zeal and talent, but this option might be impossible. Undergraduate study abroad programs are limited in the summer," Dr. Martinez said.

"Dr. Martinez, I promise you I will do whatever it takes and go wherever I need to go to make this goal of mine a reality," I replied.

Dr. Martinez smiled. He knew already how determined I was when I set a goal. He said, "Well, how about a program offered by GRIIS (Granada Institute of International Studies) at the University of Granada, Spain? Tomorrow morning I will call the director of the program."

As the hours passed, I anxiously waited to hear from Dr. Martinez about possibilities. I approached his office frequently, hoping to receive some news. Finally, he waved me into his office.

Dr. Martinez said, "I'm sorry, Laura, but I spoke to Amalia, the director of GRIIS from the University of Granada, and she told me it would be impossible for you to be part of the program. This summer Granada only offers graduate programs."

I was heartbroken at this news, but at that same moment I felt an impression on my heart as if Mother Teresa had tapped me on the shoulder and whispered in my ear: "My dear, don't worry, it is all in the Lord's hands now."

I felt a ray of light rush through every vein in my body.

"Please, Dr. Martinez, couldn't you ask her to make an exception to the rule and accept me? Couldn't you say that I was one of the most dedicated foreign language students ever in the history of Stonehill College? One who could meet the challenge of an intensive graduate program in translation and interpretation in Spanish?"

Dr. Martinez called the director of GRIIS again and highly recommended me to the graduate program even though I was an undergraduate student, only in my sophomore year of college.

He told her: "Laura Qirko is an exceptionally brilliant foreign language student possessing the greatest passion in the Spanish language that Stonehill College has ever seen."

Amalia again replied that they could not accept an undergraduate student into a graduate program. They had never done so in the history of the university. Dr. Martinez then offered Amalia the opportunity to come and meet this exceptionally brilliant student in person before reaching a final decision.

I will never forget the butterflies I had in my stomach that April day when the director of GRIIS from Spain came to Stonehill College just to meet me in person. My thoughts were: She can't accept me. I am too young, I am too inexperienced, and I am only a sophomore in college.

As all these thoughts were circulating in my mind, I felt that impression upon my heart again: "Take a deep breath my child and think positive because you are gifted and blessed from above. Be faithful always; it will lead you to success."

The moment Amalia and I made eye contact, everything changed. We started speaking in Spanish and she was very impressed with me, asking different types of questions to get to know me better. Very early in our conversation, she shook my hand and congratulated me, thereby officially accepting me into the graduate program.

"Laura, you are very special! You must have a blessing from above. Congratulations! You are the only undergraduate student to date that we have ever accepted into this graduate program," Amalia said.

Words cannot describe the joy that radiated through my entire body at that moment. I took a silent minute, looked up at the sky, smiled, and said, "Thank you, Lord! And thank you, Mother Teresa."

One of my professors and me from the GRIIS program at the University of Granada in Granada, Spain.

The summer of 2006 I traveled to Granada, Spain, and completed an intensive graduate program in translation and interpretation in four weeks. I fell in love with the Spanish language, the Spanish people, the Spanish culture, and with Spain. Because of the love that blossomed, I decided to travel to Spain each year, spending all my summers there. During the summer of 2006, I got to know Amalia and formed a more personal bond with her.

Amalia, the director of GRIIS, with my parents and me in Granada, Spain.

One day, I told Amalia the story of how I was blessed by Mother Teresa. As she listened, her eyes overflowed with tears, and she said she felt goose bumps on her arms. She said, "You just told me your story, now let me tell you mine. The moment I met you without knowing that you were blessed by Mother Teresa, I felt the spirit of God impressing upon my heart and convincing me to accept you without even really knowing you. That power reflected in your eyes the moment I met you, Laura Qirko."

People might think this was just a coincidence, but I truly believe it was Mother Teresa's blessing that made what was impossible for anyone else possible for me.

Newspaper interviews/articles about me and my successes after my return from Granada, Spain, before graduating from Stonehill College.

Mother Teresa's blessing not only helped me break records abroad but also in my new home country, the United States, throughout my college career. After having completed the summer graduate program, I was determined to push myself harder and finish my college career as a junior. This meant that my last year would consist of more than twenty courses, but I welcomed the challenge with open arms. Learning had always been a passion of mine, and graduating from Stonehill College with excellent grades became my main goal. I achieved that goal in May 2007 when I graduated summa cum laude in three years with a degree in foreign languages. The day I walked with the diploma in my hand, I looked up with the happiest smile and thanked Mother Teresa.

"Mother Teresa, forever I will be grateful to you because your blessing made my dreams come true."

Throughout my years studying at Stonehill College I was blessed with excellent professors; however, my most inspirational professor was Father James Chichetto. Father Chichetto is a priest of the Congregation of Holy Cross and an associate professor in the Communications Department at Stonehill College. Father Chichetto is one of the most humanitarian and talented people I have ever met. For four years, he worked as a missionary and educator in Peru, serving as an inspiration to other foreign students.

My three favorite professors from Stonehill College: Father Chichetto, Professor Golden, and Professor Martinez at my college graduation party in 2007.

Father Chichetto is an extremely talented author of several books of verse and prose. His work has appeared more than three hundred times in various publications, including in the Manhattan Review, the Boston Globe, Commonweal, the Boston Phoenix, the Colorado Review, America, and the London Tablet. His work has also appeared in several anthologies, including Anthology of Magazine Verse and Yearbook of American Poetry, Blood to Remember: American Poets on the Holocaust, and The Native American Anthology. He has been a recipient of numerous benefits and awards, including two NEA and three NEH grants. He is a Renaissance Weekend Scholar and is listed in The International Who's Who of Authors (Routledge), Directory of American Scholars, Mass Foundation for Humanities Scholars, Contemporary Authors Series, among others.

What made Father Chichetto such an inspiration to me was his simplicity, even though he is such a highly accomplished person. He is a simple, genuine, and generous person. Father Chichetto was not only my writing and poetry professor at Stonehill College, but he also was the person I looked up to as a role model.

He instilled in me an even deeper love and passion for writing. He was the person touched most when hearing my stories about Mother Teresa. Every day he encouraged me to pursue writing a book about my miraculous experiences with her. Father Chichetto inspired me to share my story and to spread Mother Teresa's message about becoming humanitarians with people all over the world. My last year at Stonehill College, he was my adviser in the first drafts of the first chapters of this book.

Father Chichetto was deeply touched by my story and amazed at my determination, hard work, and talent. He always told me that I was one of his best, if not the very best, student he had encountered during his teaching career.

When I graduated from Stonehill, my parents hosted an extravagant graduation party for me. Father Chichetto, as one of the guests of honor, wrote a beautiful speech, which to this day touches my heart every time I read it.

"Dear Laura,

"I will use a Morris West quote: 'We are met most powerful at crossroads and we must part each a little richer.' Your experiences at Stonehill College have taught you that service to our brothers and sisters is our highest calling. I know you have learned that from your wonderful parents. If we are going to be a happy we must live our lives in service to others while continuing to be comfortable in our personal lives and in our professional lives.

"As one of my best students, if not my best student, in twenty-five years at Stonehill College, you are exceptional. When you find yourself in a difficult situation you must ask these questions. How would I want to treat my family and friends in this situation? How would my professional colleagues judge my actions in this situation? Remember that the best gift you can give others is your example, and you have no better example than your extraordinary mother and father. Everyone arrives at the crossroads of success and failure. Common life situations bring failures, but they are not fatal. Indeed we learn from our failures. You should know that it's important to put failure behind you and then to take another step in your personal and professional journey. He or she who has never failed will never get rich in wealth or wisdom.

"At the crossroads today we realize the importance of change and transformation in our life. The words of Albert Einstein come to mind: 'to keep your balance, you must keep moving.' I know how proud your professors at Stonehill College are of you. You are our best student at Stonehill College. At the crossroads today we realize the change and transformation in our lives, we are met at the cross-roads of previous and future learning endeavors as we realize that there is more to learn. You, as a very talented multi-lingual young woman, will learn more and more each day.

"As you graduate, you are at the crossroads of the older and younger generations. It is now your turn to consider and assume responsibility so that nothing is wasted. Your love should not be wasted in hate, as your mother has taught you. Your courage should not be wasted in fear, as your mom and dad have taught you. Your wisdom should not be wasted in folly. Your beauty should not be wasted in foolishness. I'd like to think of the human existence as a mosaic. The light upon a mosaic depends upon the darkness of the shadows that surrounds it. How much light and how much shadow will there be, fortunately you can control as you evolve in your life. Your accomplishments at Stonehill College have been extraordinary, as everyone can attest to that. These are parts of your life that will help you control all aspects of life. How you react to each of the crossroads of your life will be different and it will be the light and shadow that will reflect on the mosaic in the life of your extraordinary family.

"At Stonehill College you have done so many things of service, such as helping students and providing tutorial work. I hope that in the future every step you take as you move away from Stonehill College is also the very best for you. We are met most powerful at the crossroads and we will part each a little richer and we at Stonehill College are extraordinarily rich to have had you as a student."

Laura's Reflection on
Love of Languages Breaks Records

My experience of graduating from Stonehill College in three years with a degree in three foreign languages taught me to always push myself to reach for the stars in order to achieve my dreams. Since the day I arrived in America, I have believed that I am in the land of opportunities where you can make dreams become reality with hard work and dedication. Just as I pushed myself to achieve success throughout my college years, we should always strive to do our very best. We should never give up on anything good, no matter how difficult or impossible it might seem.

We should challenge ourselves to learn more and more throughout our lives. When somebody tells us we cannot do something because it is too difficult for us, we should make every effort to prove them wrong. We must listen to our good desires. We must make the most of our time and apply wisdom to everything we do. Whether it be education or practical experience, hard work will give us hope for a successful and bright future. Nothing in life comes easy and we must work hard to achieve our goals, but when we achieve them, the result is a great feeling. We must serve as role models for the younger generations, proving that when we put our minds to it, we can achieve success.

Graduating college in three years with perfect grades, I set an example for many students. They can achieve this as well, as long as they work hard for it and believe in themselves. There is no age limit for education; some get degrees even in later years. The stars are out there, we just have to reach for them and shine like the brightest in the sky.

Study Guide Companion

❖ If you have been to college, what was it like for you? How has it changed you?

❖ Have you ever had to face a challenge that seemed difficult or impossible to you? What was the result?

❖ Are you willing to work hard to achieve your goals? How far are you willing to go?

CHAPTER 22

A HEARTFELT DECISION

After I graduated from Stonehill College, everyone wondered what I would do with my life. My goal was to use the skills I had acquired and my love of languages in the most meaningful way possible. I knew that even though I excelled as an interpreter, I had a much deeper passion. Mother Teresa had taught me to spread her message of sharing, caring, and loving one another. What better decision could I have made than to become an educator and tell children from around the world Mother Teresa's message? I followed in my mother's footsteps by becoming a high school foreign language teacher at Brockton High School.

Brockton High School, one of the largest and most diverse high schools in the United States, provided the perfect place to distribute Mother Teresa's message. Since I taught French and Spanish, I had students from all around the world from many different socioeconomic backgrounds and nationalities. I started spreading Mother Teresa's message of sharing by bringing my students chocolates, sweets, and small presents on a regular basis. My students were so inspired by these gestures that they, too, started doing the same. I demonstrated that even if we help one person, we are helping the world. Daily, I spoke to my students about the importance of community service and helping one another.

I often quoted Mother Teresa: "We ourselves feel that what we are doing is just a drop in the ocean. But the ocean would be less because of that missing drop."

Because of my encouragement, many of my students decided to volunteer. Some cleaned up parks, some painted murals, and some visited the poorest in the community. My goal was to be the best role model for my students, just as Mother Teresa was and will always be for me. This involved pushing my students to their limits whether in academics or in their personal lives. I wanted to create the best experiences for them to achieve the highest results. I encouraged them to leave footprints wherever they went—to leave a legacy in the world.

Mother Teresa made my goal a reality within my first years of teaching. I spent my summers in Spain and became the first teacher from the United States to work with one of the most important museums in Madrid: the Thyssen-Bornemisza Museum.

With the goal of improving the teaching of Spanish in the United States via social media, I, along with educational directors from the museum, created what is called a "flipped-classroom." In a flipped-classroom, the students listen to a full class lecture in Spanish directly from the educational director of the Thyssen-Bornemisza Museum. The lecture would include a piece of art or several pieces of art in an authentic setting, providing students the opportunity to use their creativity in the learning process.

With my Spanish students in my Brockton High School classroom, working on our first pilot program with Thyssen-Bornemisza Museum·

The program skyrocketed. I was invited back to Madrid to the museum for a television interview during which I discussed the success of the program for foreign language students in the United States. Because my goal is to always share good things with others, just as Mother Teresa taught me, I held several conferences in Massachusetts to inform other educators about this program and how they could link to it.

Education Director Angeles Cutillas Language during my interview in the Thyssen-Bornemisza Museum in Madrid, Spain.

Giving a lecture at the MAFLA [Massachusetts Foreign Association] to teachers from all over Massachusetts on my program with the Thyssen-Bornemisza Museum.

I am proud to say that I have linked several other schools in Massachusetts with this program. It is deeply satisfying to know that I am making a difference not only for my own students but for other foreign language students as well.

Laura's Reflection on *A Heartfelt Decision*

Following my heart and becoming a foreign language teacher taught me that if I love something very much, it is good to pursue it. It was my dream to teach languages and cultures. I had a very deep passion for working with teenagers, especially serving as a role model and inspiring them to follow their dreams just as I followed mine.

We should follow our hearts, for they can help make our dreams a reality.

If you love to heal people, then become a doctor.

If you love to help people legally, then become a lawyer.

If you have a passion for singing, then become a singer.

Don't make excuses that you can't do what you are passionate about because of other people or circumstances. If you push yourself hard and work diligently for what you want, you will be the best at what you do. Strive to challenge yourself, set bigger goals from year to year, and achieve success in what you do.

God has such an exciting plan for your life; it's beyond anything you can ever think or imagine. Read Psalms 139:1–18 and learn what God has to say about your life.

Study Guide Companion

❖ What is your greatest passion in life?

❖ What is your ideal job? How can you achieve getting this job or how did you achieve getting this job?

❖ Have you ever followed your heart in spite of obstacles and found success in what it has led you to do?

CHAPTER 23

WHAT A SURPRISE!

Since the day I met Mother Teresa, I have felt like the luckiest girl in the world. When my family and I moved to the United States, God made it our destiny to choose the city of Brockton as our hometown. At the time we didn't know that Brockton, Massachusetts, is known as the City of Champions because of one of the most famous boxing legends, the undefeated heavyweight champion Rocky Marciano.

When I found out that Rocky Marciano also called Brockton his hometown, I was proud to call myself a Brocktonian. Rocky Marciano was the boxer my father and my brother most admired. I grew up watching Rocky Marciano fights and documentaries with them.

You might wonder how a boxer could be related to Mother Teresa's message. My mother told me about one of the good deeds of this famous sportsman, which took place when he was a young boy. Rocky Marciano's father was an Italian immigrant who was working in the Brockton shoe factory to provide food for his family. Rocky decided to become a fighter in order to give back to his family what his family had worked so hard to give him. One of Rocky's main goals was to enable his father to retire. This gesture reminded me of Mother Teresa's humanitarian goals. As Mother Teresa believed: "Love begins at home, and it is not how much we do ... but how much love we put into that action."

Growing up in Brockton, I heard stories of the Marciano family, but I had never had the opportunity of meeting a member of their family. Meeting a member of the Marciano family became a dream of mine. In 2012, this fantasy was destined to become reality in a most unexpected way.

Since Brockton is Rocky Marciano's hometown, the World Boxing Federation decided to construct a twenty-foot statue of the champion in Brockton. The location of the statue was next to the Rocky Marciano Stadium, the stadium of Brockton High School, the very school that I work at as a foreign language teacher. The ceremony was set for Sunday, September 23, 2012, at noontime. Thousands of people, including boxing legends, government officials and delegations, and fans were expected to attend. I was beyond happy to be one of the fans honored to witness this event. I was counting down each day.

I will never forget the morning of September 21. As I was teaching my Spanish class, the principal of Brockton High School and the foreign language department chair came to my classroom and took me out into the hallway. A delegation of four mayors and vice mayors from Italy had just arrived in Brockton for the Rocky Marciano statue ceremony, but they did not speak English. The principal kindly asked if I could meet them at the city hall and translate for them.

Upon receiving this unexpected request, I was in shock. I knew that this opportunity could possibly make my dream a reality. Even though this was a challenge, since I had to go immediately without any preparation, I rose to the occasion and embraced that challenge with open arms. I was certain it would lead me to a great experience.

Upon arriving at Brockton City Hall, my heart was racing. I was mentally and emotionally preparing myself for this great opportunity. When I was introduced to the Italian mayors and vice mayors, I was put at ease and felt that I was destined to be there. What I thought would be a brief hour of translating at city hall turned out to be several hours of sightseeing and touring the hometown of the champion.

From left to right: Ingnazio Rucci Mayor of Ripa Teatina, Italy; me, Tod Petti, Brockton City Councilor, and Roberto Luciani, Vice Mayor of Ripa Teatina, Italy, in front of the Rocky Marciano Statue in the Rocky Marciano statue ceremony, September 23, 2012.

After leaving city hall with the Italian mayors and vice mayors, we visited Rocky Marciano's childhood home. As I was interpreting for the mayors, I felt my phone vibrating in my bag. When I checked, there was a voice message: "Where are you, Laura? Isn't school over for today?" As we were leaving Rocky Marciano's home, they asked if I would accompany the Italian mayors as a guest and interpreter at the dinner ceremonies held the entire weekend of the Rocky Marciano statue ceremony. These dinners were only for the Marciano family, state officials, and delegations from Mexico. These included the president of the World Boxing Federation, the artists who had designed and constructed the beautiful Rocky Marciano statue, and several world renowned legendary boxers. I was also told to invite my parents to attend all the festivities. Not believing what I was hearing, I managed to drive myself home to astonish my parents.

As I parked my car in the driveway, I saw my mother and father waiting outside the house. They were clearly worried about me. The moment I stepped out of the car, my mother said, "Laura where have you been? It's almost six in the afternoon and I have called you more than ten times and have received no answer from you. We were worried sick about you!"

I replied, "Mom, if I tell you where I have been until now, you will not believe me. The only thing I will tell you is you have fifteen minutes to get ready to start the weekend of a lifetime!"

As I was explaining to my parents the surprise, they could hardly believe what they were hearing. My mother's eyes filled with tears of joy and my father's smile lit up the room. He was overwhelmed that his dream was coming true. He was going to meet Rocky Marciano's family and several famous boxers whom he had admired for years.

Rocky Marciano Jr., Rocky Marciano's son, in front of his father's statue in his grandfather's hometown of Ripa Teatina, Italy.

During the Rocky Marciano statue ceremony dinner, I met the son of the undefeated heavyweight champion. When we were introduced, I felt a shock wave run through me and I felt we were destined to become real friends. I felt an impression upon my heart as I translated in front of thousands of people and heard a small, quiet voice say, "My dear, this joyous occasion is only the start of what will be a lifelong bond with the Rocky Marciano family!"

The words impressed upon my heart started to become reality the moment the mayors from Italy told the guests at the ceremony that in honor of Rocky Marciano every year during the summer they have an event called Premio Rocky Marciano, during which they award prizes to famous Italian athletes in Rocky Marciano's name. This happens in Ripa Teatina, Italy, the birthplace of Rocky Marciano's father.

They informed us that for the upcoming Premio Rocky Marciano 2013, they would be honored to have Rocky Marciano Jr. attend as the guest of honor, accompanied by me as his interpreter and a delegation from Rocky Marciano's hometown of Brockton, Massachusetts.

After I translated for the Italian mayors for three consecutive days during the Rocky Marciano statue ceremony, I decided I would follow Mother Teresa's footsteps and dedicate all my hard work to the city of Brockton by doing all the work free of charge. What a joy to know that I was making my home city proud and setting an example of charity on this big occasion for our city.

For the few free hours the Italian mayors had during the Rocky Marciano festivities, my family and I decided to take them on an exclusive tour of the beautiful city of Boston and also honor them by taking them to lunch at Boston's premier restaurant, The Top of the Hub. Their last night in Brockton, I took them out to dinner to an Italian restaurant to make them feel close to home even though they were thousands of miles away.

The last morning they spent in Brockton, my mother invited them to our house for what they described as the "most unforgettable brunch of their lives." To our blessed family who dedicates their time into doing for others, it was a great pleasure to welcome these new friends with open arms. As I was saying goodbye to them, they reminded me that when they invited Rocky Marciano Jr. to Italy, they would invite me as well as the interpreter.

The brunch at my house with the mayor and vice mayor of Ripa Teatina, Ignazio Rucci and Roberto Luciani. September 24, 2012.

As the months passed, I began to think it would never happen; it was just an impossible dream. Unexpectedly in March 2013, I received a phone call from the vice mayor of Ripa Teatina inviting Rocky Marciano Jr. and me as guests of honor to Premio Rocky Marciano 2013.

The summer of 2013 was terrific, indeed, since it was the first year I had the privilege of accompanying Rocky Marciano Jr. to Italy for Premio Rocky Marciano 2013.

From the moment I arrived in Italy, I felt very fortunate for this wonderful experience. Imagine a high school teacher suddenly having personal chauffeurs; a private villa to stay in; five-course meals each day; a personal hair and makeup artist; and, most importantly, translating for several television and newspaper interviews as well as in front of thousands of people at the Premio Rocky Marciano.

I truly felt special during the Premio Rocky Marciano 2013 as I translated for Rocky Marciano Jr. I have been fortunate and blessed to meet many people from around the world; Rocky Marciano Jr. is surely one of them. He is such a genuine, sweet, loving, caring, respectful, and intelligent man. What I thought would be just a very formal business relationship with him turned out to be one of the most precious friendships in my life. I dearly cherish him.

As I tell Rocky Jr., I have an older biological brother named Dritan, but I also have a special brother named Rocky Marciano Jr. I believe Mother Teresa's encouraging words to a young girl played a key role in making this dream come true.

Premio Rocky Marciano 2015 held another great surprise. In April 2015, Rocky Marciano Jr. told me that the Marcellino family wanted to make a major movie about the life of Rocky Marciano and the producer of the movie, Mr. Yochanan Marcellino, would be joining us in Italy as the guest of honor for Premio Rocky Marciano 2015.

When I arrived in Rome, Mr. Marcellino was waiting for me at the airport. The moment we met, I felt the same feeling rush through my body and that gentle, quiet voice say, "My dear, this is a very special person who will be part of your life as a lifelong friend."

Yochanan Marcellino and me the first minutes we met in the Fiumicino Airport in Rome, Italy, 2015.

I can truly say that one of the kindest persons I have ever met is the movie producer, Mr. Yochanan Marcellino. I was honored to be accompanying and interpreting for him during his one-week stay in Italy. That was the year Rocky Marciano Jr., Yochanan Marcellino, and I formed a bond around our love for Rocky Marciano.

Yochanan Marcellino, Rocky Marciano Jr., and me in Ripa Teatina, Italy, 2015.

In Italy that year I got very much involved in different types of interviews regarding the movie, and setting up some important meetings regarding that film. Mr. Marcellino would joke around with me, saying, "Laura, you are great at being my personal manager! That is what I will call you, the manager!"

I took that to heart and dedicated all the time that I could to whatever was needed for the making of the movie. This involved translating various interviews, translating Italian music, and translating in general as we traveled back and forth to Italy, filming behind-the-scenes footage from Ripa Teatina.

Since Rocky Marciano was from Brockton, the majority of the movie will be filmed there; however, there is a small part that Yochanan wants to film in Italy, right on the streets of Ripa Teatina with the local people.

I am extremely happy to be working with the movie entitled Undefeated, by translating from English into Italian or Italian into English. From the time I was a little girl, my talents have been acting and speaking foreign languages. I was fascinated by movies, especially foreign movies. My love for cinema was part of what inspired me to pursue a career in foreign languages. Throughout my entire foreign language career, I have never forgotten my deep love for cinema.

Little did I know that my passion for foreign languages would lead me to become a professional translator in the movie industry. If it wasn't for my Italian, I would never be involved in what I predict to be a Box Office International Hit. I am truly blessed from above.

I have been accompanying Rocky Marciano Jr. to Ripa Teatina year after year. Traveling to Italy as a personal interpreter is a lot of fun, but it can also be difficult and stressful. Not only do I have to work all day and all night translating on the spot whether for formal interviews or simple conversation, but it also requires translating long speeches onstage in front of thousands of people. Even though when interpreters first take on a job, the first thing they think about is signing a contract, when I go to Italy, that is the last thought in my mind.

Me translating on stage for Yochanan Marcellino and Rocky Marciano Jr. at the Premio Rocky Marciano 2015, Ripa Teatina, Italy.

I decided to dedicate all my work to the people of Ripa Teatina; therefore, I preferred to do this free of charge. The money I could earn while working there, I would rather see used for things like building schools or fixing roads in Ripa Teatina. That is much more important than taking the money and using it for myself. After all, I am not doing anything special, I am just following Mother Teresa's footsteps by being the best humanitarian I can be.

The town of Ripa Teatina, Italy.

I have formed very strong bonds with many of the people in Ripa Teatina, even to the point that I consider them as family. Since the first year I returned from Ripa Teatina, during Christmas time I send every family I know a Christmas present and a Christmas card with money. My mother and I set aside some money to do something like this for families in Ripa Teatina, especially those with young children.

When I return to Ripa Teatina in the summer, I bring presents for each and every member of the families I know, as well as giving them some money to help them in whatever small way I can. I have invited all my friends from Ripa Teatina to come to Brockton. For the few that have come, I have made sure to make their trips unforgettable. I take them to many places and also buy them presents.

There is no greater joy than seeing others happy. When I see others happy, I feel double the happiness myself. Also, by doing this, I am setting a good example for them that there is nothing more beautiful than doing the best you can for others. This is a message I strive to share around the world throughout all my life.

CHAPTER 24

ROCKY MARCIANO WINE

Ever since I was blessed by Mother Teresa, one of my deepest passions has become connecting people to create successful relationships. I was given this opportunity in one of the most unique ways. In 2013, the first year Rocky Marciano Jr. and I were in Italy, the Cantina of Ripa Teatina (Winery of Ripa Teatina) offered Rocky Jr. the opportunity to create a wine in honor of his father. The wine was to be made in Ripa Teatina, the land of Rocky Marciano's father.

Rocky Jr. gladly accepted this special offer and was thrilled to honor his father in such a prestigious way. When we returned to Italy the following year in 2014, Rocky told me that he had heard about one of the best wineries in Abruzzo, Italy, the Masciarelli Winery. Rocky Jr. did not know that for years the owners of the Masciarelli Winery and I had had a very special bond in Boston. When we were in Italy that year, Rocky Jr., myself, and a few friends went to visit the Masciarelli Winery. When we arrived there, Rocky Jr. was very impressed with everything about the winery and immediately fell in love with it.

Rocky Jr. and me in the Masciarelli Winery in Abruzzo, Italy, in 2014.

When I saw the happiness in his eyes, I said, "Rocky, do you know that the owner of the Masciarelli Winery is a very dear friend of mine in Boston? As a matter of fact, I will one day make your wish of meeting her and her family come true when you come to Boston."

Rocky's wish was granted when Rocky Jr. visited Boston in 2016 to speak with potential distributors for his father's wine in Massachusetts. Rocky Jr. met and spoke with many distributors; however, his greatest wish was to potentially work with the Masciarelli's as the distributors. Rocky Jr. asked me a huge favor, to connect him with the owner, Anna Masciarelli.

I had for years talked to Anna Masciarelli about how wonderful Rocky Marciano Jr. was and how special he was to me, and I had also been speaking to Rocky Jr. of how sweet and loving Anna Masciarelli was. It was as if the two were destined to meet. As soon Rocky Marciano Jr. and Anna Masciarelli met, it was "love at first sight"—the love a grandmother would feel for a grandson. Rocky said, "The minute I hugged Anna Masciarelli, it felt like I was giving a warm hug to my Italian grandmother."

Words cannot describe the joy I felt to witness this beautiful, special bond. Rocky decided that day that the Masciarelli's were meant to be the distributors of the wine. I absolutely loved being the person who made a dream connection reality.

Laura, Rocky Jr. and Anna Masciarelli in the Masciarelli Winery in Boston, 2014.

This connection was just the first connection I would make for Rocky Jr. regarding the Rocky Marciano wine. In September 2017, Rocky Jr. decided to launch the Rocky Marciano wine in his father's home state of Massachusetts. The moment Rocky Jr. told me about this, I started planning. Because of the unconditional love I feel for Rocky Jr., I wanted to make sure that this wine debut was as successful as possible. I took it upon myself to contact different owners of some of the best Italian restaurants in the Boston area. I wanted Rocky Jr. to make connections with the best people possible for his business to start to bloom in Massachusetts.

The first wine dinner I set up was at a restaurant named Luciano's. The owner Luciano Canova, a dear friend of mine, had heard me speak highly of Rocky Jr. for years. This was the best opportunity to introduce them. Luciano is a passionate Italian immigrant who has had tremendous success in the restaurant business in the United States. He was one of the best people to introduce Rocky Jr. to for guidance.

The wine dinner at Luciano's was one of the most unforgettable dinners of my life.

Owner of Luciano's restaurant , Luciano Canova, and Rocky Marciano Jr. at Luciano's for the launch of Rocky Marciano wine, September 2016.

Rocky Marciano Jr. and me at Luciano's restaurant for the launch of the Rocky Marciano wine, September 2016.

Hannah Marcellino, Yochanan Marcellino, and Rocky Marciano Jr. at Luciano's for the launch of Rocky Marciano wine, September 2016.

Laura Qirko, ambassador of Rocky Marciano wine at its launch at the 2016 Masciarelli Wine Show at the Boston Harbor Hotel, September 2016.

Rocky Jr. was honored with the presence of Yochanan Marcellino and his wife, Hannah, who had flown all the way from Nashville, Tennessee, just to show their support and love for Rocky Jr. Yochanan and Hannah are two of the dearest people to Rocky Jr. and me. That night it felt like we were a happy family joyfully celebrating in a beautiful atmosphere with delicious food, the very best company and last but not least the Rocky Marciano wine.

During the launch of the Rocky Marciano wine, I took on the role of the ambassador for Rocky Marciano wine in Massachusetts. I attended the Masciarelli Wine Show at the Boston Harbor Hotel in Boston where I introduced the wine to hundreds of restaurant owners. When the launch of the Rocky Marciano wine weekend was over, my job had just begun. I connected Rocky Jr. with restaurants such as Alma Nove, the Top of the Hub, and Sabatino's. My goal was to call the owners or managers of these restaurants and introduce the wine to them by connecting them with Rocky Marciano Jr.'s special story.

I did this for weeks and weeks during my free time for charity and, without any compensation but with the greatest pleasure. A lot of people questioned why I would do such a difficult and time-consuming task free of charge. My answer always was "sacrificial love."

Mother Teresa taught me that sacrificial love is the best gift we can give to the people dear to our hearts. Rocky Marciano Jr. holds a very special place in my heart; therefore, I did all of this for him with the greatest pleasure. I love connecting good people because I believe the more good people I connect; the more that good people will connect with me. In keeping with the teachings of Mother Teresa, every good deed is viewed and valued by Jesus; therefore, when a door of opportunity opens, I enter with open arms.

Laura's Reflection on
What a Surprise!/Rocky Marciano Wine

Having the opportunity to be the interpreter of the son of the world-famous boxer Rocky Marciano taught me that the best things in life happen when you least expect them. In a million years, I would never have imagined that one day God would hand me this opportunity. I was courageous enough to accept it without thinking twice and to welcome it with open arms.

I knew it would be extremely challenging, but I knew that only good things were to follow.

We must believe that when we accept a huge challenge, within our capabilities, the end result will be a very good one. When we are handed a special opportunity, we should take it. For me it was difficult at first because all I could think about was that I had not used my Italian language skills for years; however, I pushed myself from my former background knowledge to build on it. I knew that I had to push myself with the grammar by using my French grammar background.

For example, if you are an architect and you have only constructed small individual homes and now you have the opportunity of constructing a skyscraper, at first you might be fearful because you might feel that you don't have the required knowledge. You need to use the background knowledge you have in constructing a house and build upon it and learn more going from there. You should not turn down an offer because you fear it is too difficult; you should rise to the challenge because only good things are to follow. Who could have thought that by taking up the opportunity to translate for Rocky Jr. would give me the opportunity to be involved in translating for a major movie production? This taught me that the best things in life come when you least expect them but only if you accept them with open arms.

Study Guide Companion

❖ Do you believe that the best things in life come when you least expect them?

❖ What opportunity in life have you taken that you were rewarded for?

❖ Do you believe that your hard work will bring you success?

CHAPTER 25

GUARDIAN ANGELS

The greatest lesson Mother Teresa taught us was to be the best humanitarians by helping people whenever we can. By helping even one person, we are changing the world. It is a wonderful feeling to know we made a difference for the better in someone's life. It is not important to do great things, but it is important to put love into every "little" thing we do.

Our family has helped people all around the world, but I want to tell you the story about a girl named Roubina, who thinks of us as her guardian angels.

In the summer of 2009, during our visit to Granada, Spain, one evening my mother, father, and I decided to call my brother in the United States from one of the phone booths located inside a small souvenir shop. At the shop I asked a beautiful young girl who was working there how much our phone call would cost. When she started speaking, I knew immediately from her accent that she was an immigrant.

Rubina the day we met her in the souvenir shop in Granada, Spain.

She was from Syria and had immigrated to Spain along with her husband, who was studying at the university there. She told us about how hard it had been to leave behind her entire family, including her beloved parents, for a better future in Spain. My mother and I told her the story of our immigration to the United States. We understood her struggles, we felt her pain, because just like her we were once immigrants.

My mother was brought up to think that when you meet someone who is struggling, you should not judge them. You must simply show them love. My mother and I looked at each other and, in Albanian, I said, "Let's bring some presents to this young woman."

We did not really know her, but we knew that for sure our gesture would touch her heart. We returned to our apartment, which was only a two-minute walk from the shop, to pick out presents for her. I chose a few of my brand-new dresses to give her since we were approximately the same size and seemed to be about the same age.

When we returned to the shop with these things, she began crying. She could not believe that these were presents for her; they seemed to come out of nowhere! In Spanish she said, "How is it possible that you—strangers who just met me in this store and don't even know me—are giving me these gifts?"

"Unfortunately we are leaving tomorrow for the United States, but we will come and say goodbye," we told her.

When we stopped by the shop the next day, we brought with us our remaining Spanish money, about forty dollars. We knew that even though this was not a lot, it would be a great help to her because we kept on thinking about her immigrant struggles, struggles we had once experienced.

When Roubina saw us coming, she rushed out of the store to give us each a hug.

"Roubina, please take this money to buy some food for your family. We know this money is not going to change your life, but it will give you hope that there are people in this world who will encourage and help you build a successful life," we said.

When she saw the money, she fell on her knees crying and saying, "God, I can't believe this. No one has ever done this for me. No one has ever cared for me like you two. God must be very big to send me such an unexpected blessing by bringing generous people like you into my life. You are truly my guardian angels sent from above and I will always be thankful to you."

The tears flowing down her cheeks, as she was saying goodbye to us, are tears we will never forget.

My mother gave her another hug and said, "Don't worry, Roubina, next summer when we return to Granada, we will come to see you again."

In haste to leave, however, we forgot to exchange addresses and phone numbers needed to contact her after we returned home.

My mother and I were positive that when we returned to Granada in the summer, we would go back to the same shop and find her there. So throughout the year we bought presents to take to her when we saw her again. We knew that being an Islamic Syrian woman was not easy. Roubina must have been facing a very difficult time. We decided that we must help her because even though many people would look at her as an insignificant Muslim girl from Syria, to us she was a sweet, precious human being. We were not impressed by her religion; we were impressed by her heart. My mother and I wanted to set an example that charity transcends religious differences.

The next summer my mother, father, and I returned to Granada hoping to find Roubina and deliver the many presents we had gathered for her. Even though we had not been in contact for a year, we still were hopeful we could surprise her with our visit. As we happily arrived at the shop, not only was she not there that day, we were told that she no longer worked there. The owners had no idea where she was.

I told my mother, "See, Mom, I was afraid this was going to happen, that we were not going to find Roubina this year!"

My mother replied, "Laura, don't give up hope; I know we will find her. I have a strong feeling that very soon we will find her when we don't expect it. "

My mother's words must have gone directly to God's ears because that same afternoon as we were leaving our apartment to go out for the evening, I heard someone call my name: "Laura! Laura!"

When I turned around, there was Roubina, who was working right next to our apartment. Because she was an immigrant, she was let go from her job she had the previous year and had started to work at another souvenir shop to earn money her family needed for food.

She was so happy to see her family from the United States that she immediately invited us to her home.

"I have been waiting for this moment for one year, counting down each day. You have brought such happiness and I would be honored if you would accept a dinner invitation to a poor girl's home," she said.

"Yes, it will be our greatest pleasure!" we joyfully replied.

We went to Roubina's place, where she and her husband lived in very difficult conditions. It was a small one-bedroom apartment that was very poorly furnished. But what caught our attention was the royal display of food that she had prepared with love. Her face shined as if she were the richest girl in the world to have us in her presence and share a meal as one family. That night we showered her with presents from the United States and gave her two hundred dollars for herself and her husband and two hundred dollars for her parents back home who were also very poor.

Roubina and my mother the moment they reunited at the new souvenir shop in Granada, Spain, the day she invited us for dinner.

She started to weep and said, "I feel so blessed to have my mother, my father, and my sister from America who love me and have not only brought me such beautiful things but also came to visit me. Today I will share with you the happiest news that I'm pregnant. Mama, you have brought me luck since the day you touched me and I have a feeling that the child I am carrying will be a blessed child."

When we heard this joyful news, my mother said: "Roubina, I don't want you to worry about buying anything for the baby. As soon as Laura and I return to the United States, we will buy you everything you will need for the baby—all the baby clothes and other essentials. We will send you a package on a weekly basis so that by the time the baby is born the baby will have everything ready awaiting him or her with love. The only things we cannot mail are the crib and baby furniture pieces, so I will send you the money via Western Union to buy and furnish the baby room."

How happy my mother was to "adopt" this baby by buying gifts for a child whose grandmother was so far away.

Roubina was so overwhelmed that she knelt down to my mother, kissing her hand while praying to God: "God, I will forever be grateful to you for bringing into my life my guardian angel. This woman is truly my second mother. I will be thankful all the days of my life for this gift you have blessed me with. Mama Marjeta will be in my heart every day when I wake up and every night when I go to sleep. You have blessed this child that I am carrying by showing him or her the true meaning of unconditional love. I will forever be grateful to you, God."

As soon as we arrived home in the United States, we kept the promise we made to Roubina by buying her everything the baby would need all the way through his toddler years. We bought bodysuits, shirts, pants, socks, shoes, sneakers, hats, gloves, jackets, blankets, towels, and of course lots of baby toys. Week after week my mother would send Roubina a package containing more than twenty baby items. And we sent her money to buy a crib. This baby was showered with blessings from the Qirko women.

The next summer my mother and I returned to Granada, thrilled to meet the three-month-old baby boy, Mekdad. From the moment the baby saw my mother, he kept looking and smiling at her. He held on tightly to her with his tiny hand and would not let go. He was the most tranquil and happy baby we had ever seen. We visited him every day and he became very attached to us.

My mother with baby Mekdad in Roubina's house in Granada, Spain.

Mekdad and me on a nightly stroll through the streets of Granada, Spain. He is wearing the Boston Red Socks outfit I bought for him.

When my mother and I were not able to visit him for a few days, Roubina told us that he cried and cried as he looked at the door in hopes of seeing us. It was as if he was missing us and felt a strong spiritual connection with us because we had done so much for him.

One year later, we returned again to Granada and Mekdad had just started talking and walking. In his cute baby voice he would call me "Laura," call my mother *"Abuela,"* which in Spanish means grandma, and call my father *"Abuelo,"* which in Spanish means grandpa. Even at such a young age, he felt we were part of his family. We might not have been connected by blood, but we were connected by heart.

That year when my mother was giving him gifts, he would kiss her hands and arms without anyone telling him to do so. He would say, *"Gracias, Abuela, te quiero!,"* which in Spanish means "Thank you, Grandma, I love you." He truly felt love in his heart and expressed it through his actions. We have continued to shower gifts on that boy and his family for more than eight years. For his "guardian angels," he is and will always be our little blessed boy.

Mekdad, three years old, in his house in Granada, Spain.

Our precious little boy picks up his mother's phone and talks to us on a weekly basis. At only five years old, he said, "Thank you, Grandma Marjeta and Auntie Laura, for continuing to help us with clothes and money for food. I love everything you send me because you send everything with love. I love you very much and I miss you very much. I want you to come to my house as soon as possible because I want to give you a big hug and kiss."

Roubina had another baby boy in April 2017; his name is Nazim. We are following our mission of being "guardian angels" for this baby too. We are continuing to do good deeds just as Mother Teresa taught us. The more love we give to people, the more love we will receive, especially precious when it comes from a child.

As Mother Teresa taught us, love is the greatest gift we can give to one another. Again, it is not how much we do but how much love we put into our actions. Let our actions serve as a message to everyone in the world that joy comes with a smile.

Laura's Reflection on *Guardian Angels*

Being guardian angels to an immigrant Syrian Muslim woman in Spain has taught me that it is such a great feeling knowing you changed someone's life. There is nothing better than doing charity for people who need it the most. I learned that we should always help our brothers and sisters whenever they are in need. We should provide food or money for food for the needy, regardless of their nationality or religion. We have to set an example of religious tolerance. We should not judge someone based on their religion, we should welcome that person for who he or she is.

My mother and I decided to help Roubina because she was a young immigrant in a foreign land where she faced many forms of discrimination. Discrimination is an issue that touches our heart at its core because we, too, were immigrants in the United States. Even though as immigrants in the United States, we were fortunate not to face discrimination, we understand the struggles other immigrants face in other countries. At the same time, we can appreciate whatever help is provided to us in moments of need.

Our passion has become reaching out and helping immigrants no matter their nationality, race, or religion. By helping immigrants, we are helping nations; by helping nations, we are helping the world; by helping the world, we are serving God by showing His love and becoming true humanitarians.

Study Guide Companion

❖ Have you ever helped someone of a different background who needed help? How has that experience changed your life?

❖ How does your conception of the world change when you witness charity?

❖ Have you ever witnessed discrimination against an immigrant or any other person? How did you respond to what you witnessed?

CHAPTER 26

HEALING HANDS

One of the most special blessings that Mother Teresa gave my mother was when she held my mother's hands and prayed for my mother to receive the spiritual gift of healing administered through the laying on of hands. Mother Teresa believed and operated in that gifting. God gave my mother this special gift in Jesus' name, to see a miraculous change in people's lives after simply praying for them. Throughout the years, my mother has prayed the prayer Mother Teresa taught her when praying for suffering people.

My mother's prayer usually consists of these words: "Dear Jesus, I pray to You with all my heart as You are the only one who performs miracles. Please heal this person who is suffering. Let him [or her] be free of pain, free of illness, and full of good health. Jesus, it is You who performs miracles through Your grace. To You I pray, my Lord. Amen!"

My mother's obedience in the laying on of hands, along with her childlike faith that Jesus is hearing her prayers and interceding for the person who is suffering, have often resulted in people experiencing healing in their bodies from the smallest health problems, such as headaches, to very serious health issues such as a terminal illness.

My mother has always used homeopathic remedies for our family's ailments. The biggest miracle for me that Jesus performed through the laying on of hands by my mother took place when a huge lump appeared underneath my arm when I was twenty years old. It started out as a small pimple or bite and as each day passed, it got bigger and bigger and I was in almost unbearable pain. My mother touched it every day and prayed.

"Don't worry, Laura, because very soon God will take all the bad inside and make it go away," she said.

I did not understand why every day she would tell me to put directly on the lump a slice of tomato with sugar on it. My mother said that the tomato acid combined with the sugar would suck up the puss from the infection and make it explode. But as the pain was becoming unbearable, I decided to go to the doctor and have this enormous lump surgically removed. Since my mother could not bear the pain of seeing a knife cutting through me, the night before the doctor's appointment, my mother kept praying the words Mother Teresa taught her as she softly touched my wound.

That morning, one hour before we went to the hospital for the surgery, my mother prayed that the puss would explode so she could remove the lump herself. I thought my mother was completely delusional to think that this large lump would somehow magically explode, but to my surprise, that is exactly what happened. The puss exploded like a volcano and my mother squeezed and drained the entire lump. After screaming from the top of my lungs, all of a sudden I felt calm as I looked at my wound, which seemed as if there had never been anything there.

When we went to the hospital, the doctor examined the place the lump had been and was amazed at how everything was cured. Shocked, he said, "Laura, you need to thank your mother for saving you from surgery."

After taking several tests and getting excellent results, the doctor said, "I have no words other than that your mother is a miracle healer with a blessing from above."

Another miracle my mother performed was for my father. Several years ago, the doctors told my father that he had a stone in his urinary canal. Because of the position of the stone, my father's prostate had enormously enlarged. According to the doctors, this was a very dangerous situation and because there was no way to shrink the stone, the only option was to surgically remove it.

Since my father is petrified of anything to do with surgery, upon hearing the word surgery, he started to panic. As the time for the surgery approached, my father's fear increased. My mother said, "Fred, I will pray that the stone little by little breaks up before you go into surgery, so that they don't have to operate on you. All you have to do is listen to what I tell you do, eat what I give you, and remain positive."

My mother is fortunate to know a lot of effective homeopathic remedies, and every day she gave my father as many remedies as she could to improve the chances of naturally breaking up the stone. His diet for one week consisted of watermelon, pumpkin seeds, and the juice of boiled corn husks and asparagus. Each time she prepared him the food, she would say her Mother Teresa prayer.

The day my parents went to the hospital for the surgery, the doctors were astonished to find out that not only had the stone completely broken up, but the prostate was back to its normal size as well. The doctors cancelled the surgery and removed all the small stone pieces with a quick ultra-wave procedure. The doctors were amazed and called this incident "two miracles in one day," true miracles that they had never witnessed before. Mother Teresa's prayer is truly wonderful and God used it to help save my father from surgery.

***

Recently in Italy my mother's gift was used in a special way to bring God's healing touch to people suffering from three different conditions, just by praying for them and laying on her hands.

The first example was the world-famous boxing champion Rocky Mattioli. Rocky Mattioli is an Italian boxer who lived in Australia for the majority of his life and has now permanently moved back to Italy. Ripa Teatina is his hometown. He is a guest of honor each year at the Premio Rocky Marciano.

Throughout his boxing career he suffered a lot with his shoulders, and now in his sixties and fully retired, he is feeling the effects of boxing on his body. Rocky could not lift his shoulders because of chronic pain that prevented him from even raising his arms. He asked my mother if she could lay her hands on his shoulders and pray for him because even after constant years of therapy and medical treatment nothing seemed to relieve his pain.

My mother praying for healing for boxer
Rocky Mattioli in Ripa Teatina, Italy.

My mother laid her hands on his shoulders and started to pray for him with Mother Teresa's healing prayer. She said, "Rocky, close your eyes and pray with positive thoughts because part of the healing process is positive thinking."

Within five minutes of receiving a shoulder massage from my mother, Rocky started to feel some relief. He thanked her and told her that he had honestly never felt that good for decades. After one year passed, when we met him again, the first thing he said to my mother as he gave her a warm hug and kiss was, "Marjeta, you are truly a miracle healer and a blessed saint because ever since you touched my shoulders last year, I no longer have the horrific pain I have had throughout the past years of my life."

These words made my mother so joyful!

***

Another miracle God performed through my mother also happened in Italy. When my parents and I were there in 2016, an Italian friend of mine told me that her elderly sister had been very sick for years and that her health had deteriorated during the past few months. As I listened to her touching story, I decided to tell her about how God used my mother's healing touch on suffering people.

"Laura," she begged, her eyes filled with tears of desperation, "would it be possible for your mother to meet my sister in person and pray for her the way you have been telling me works?"

My mother welcomed the sick woman with open arms in hopes of God performing a miracle. My mother touched the woman's head, neck, and spine, since she suffered from problems in those areas due to cervical spondylosis. As my mother touched these places, she prayed a special prayer that Mother Teresa gave her.

After finishing the massage, the woman thanked my mother from the bottom of her heart and, in Italian, with a big smile of hope told us that she felt as if Mother Teresa were touching her and praying for her. A few hours after this, I received a message from this woman's sister: "Laura, please thank your mother again because my sister said she started to feel a difference the moment your mother laid hands on her."

A few days after this, I received another message: "Laura, my sister is feeling so much better! She has never felt this good for years and years!"

After a month had passed since we returned from Italy, I received another message from this woman: "My sister, thanks to your mother, is doing excellently and is pain free. Do you remember how desperate and hopeless she was? Now because of your mother she is transformed into a different person and for this I will never stop thanking God for your mother. Your mother is truly God's instrument for healing in the name of Jesus."

In the same message, she said: "Could I ask another huge favor from your mother? I have a very dear friend whose daughter is terminally ill in the hospital. She has been fighting a brain tumor for many years. She recently got married in 2013 and has a beautiful child. I could not resist asking your mother to say a prayer for her since I have witnessed with my own eyes that her prayers are used to bring about a miracle touch from God. I know your mother must be in person to lay hands on her, but if I give you her name, your mother can see a photo of her on Facebook as she prays for her health. I just saw a movie about Mother Teresa on television and could not help thinking of the Mother Teresa I personally know—your mother Marjeta!"

This was truly a touching message regarding the power of healing through prayer and the laying on of hands in Jesus' name.

Laura's Reflection on *Healing Hands*

Witnessing God healing people through my mother's hands in prayer taught me that healing miracles can happen when we pray earnestly to God. Jesus performs miracles through our prayers. We should always pray to Him to heal us from whatever we are suffering from and be thankful to Him for everything He does. If we believe in Him and pray to Him, then miracles are possible.

These experiences also made me a believer in natural healers all around the world. In the world we live in, there are two options when it comes to healing, either synthetic medication or homeopathic remedies. Witnessing miracles performed by my mother's hands, combining prayer with homeopathic remedies, made me understand that this is a valid form of healing. The combination of homeopathic remedies and a strong belief in and prayer to God can perform miracles in our lives.

Study Guide Companion

❖ Do you believe in the power of healing through prayer to God?

❖ Have you ever been healed from a health problem? How has that experience changed you?

❖ Have you ever used homeopathic remedies? Describe that experience.

CHAPTER 27

BLESSED BREAD

One of the most important things Mother Teresa discussed with us the day we met her was that bread is the most blessed and sacred thing in the world. She told us to always cherish and be thankful for our daily bread and to never throw bread away without reflecting that there are thousands of people all around the world who go hungry every day because of the lack of bread. This message struck my mother to her heart's core because my grandmother had also taught her the same message when she was a little child.

My mother decided that she would combine her love of bread with her special gift, the prayer that Mother Teresa taught her to share this message with everyone that came across her path. Since my mother was blessed by Mother Teresa, she started to make what she calls her "blessed bread" after moving to the United States in 1995. My mother makes a very special type of bread, bread you cannot purchase in any store.

My mother Marjeta, baking her blessed bread.

What makes her bread truly different is not the size, not the texture, not the taste, but the blessing she bestows upon it. As my mother makes the bread, she also blesses the bread, finishing it off with a cross. She prays the special prayer Mother Teresa taught her in order to bless the bread. The people fortunate enough to eat my mom's bread will receive a special blessing because of the love poured into the bread.

At Brockton High School my mother decided to spread Mother

Teresa's message about sharing our daily bread by bringing freshly baked bread every day to the main office in order to bless all the people who ate it. At Brockton High School, the minute the name Marjeta Qirko is mentioned, people remember she is the remarkable woman who makes the blessed bread.

My mother's blessed bread fresh out of the oven.

***

My mother decided to put together a very special lunch for more than 650 people at Brockton High School when she retired in 2009. My mother and I went shopping and spent more than five thousand dollars on food for the lunch. We felt that was the best money we could have spent because it left a strong imprint on peoples' minds. My mother and I cooked for more than three days to assure we had made enough food for everyone. As my mother prepared the food, she also blessed the food in order to bring blessings to everyone who ate it.

My mother in one of the four cafeterias in Brockton High School the day of the lunch she prepared.

My mother with the principal of Brockton High School and the superintendent of Brockton Public Schools at her retirement party in June 2009.

The day my mother retired, the principal of Brockton High School said, "Marjeta Qirko has done something no one in the history of Brockton High School has ever done before. She prepared a blessed spread for more than 650 people in order to bring us the same blessings Mother Teresa brought to her. For all of us, she is the best example of a noble humanitarian just like Mother Teresa."

My mother and Gloria Rubilar at my mother's retirement party in 2009.

My mother was deeply touched by all the beautiful heartfelt letters, cards, and messages that hundreds of colleagues and students wrote to her. Though there are too many to include here, I would like to share a letter that one of my mother's fellow colleagues and best friends, Gloria Rubliar, a Spanish teacher and guidance counselor at Brockton High School wrote for her.

"Once reading to my children Mother Teresa's words about loving and giving, I stopped to say to them I do know one person like that and her name is Marjeta. She has a smile for everyone, she will comfort and help those who are in need, not hesitating in giving her time, her own money or food if that is what is required in order to do it. She knows that if somebody needs help or is going through a difficult time, she will approach him or her to help. Marjeta shares the bread with everyone. Yes! Literally she does. She makes every morning her own blessed bread, which she shares with everyone, including administrators, teachers, janitors, and her own students. As a teacher, she gives life-skills lessons to her students. There is no teaching topic she would not use to encourage her students to help each other, to accept each other, to share with each other, being herself a role model for all those students. I had the

*wonderful opportunity of knowing Marjeta Qirko. I feel blessed to
have her friendship. She is not like anyone I have met before.*

*"What else can be said about a woman like Marjeta Qirko? I only
know that I could barely wash her feet if I was given the opportunity to do it. I was brought up as a Catholic. As an adult I opened
my mind to other ways to look for God, for the same reason I have
attended many different churches and congregations. I came to the
conclusion that I was being so selfish all the time thinking that I
was following Christ's words, but really I was looking for my own
conformity, saving myself, discriminating against others, and going
home right after the service. Then I met Marjeta, my entire vision
of what giving, loving, and unselfishness was changed 360 degrees.
She just does, is, and lives the most authentic Christian life a God's
child could live."*

(My mother didn't interpret what Gloria said to mean that following
Mother Teresa is wonderful but being a Catholic is selfish. There are innu-
merable wonderful Catholics who give generously to the poor.)

Other colleagues wrote the following messages:

*"Marjeta has never ceased to amaze me with her energy, determi-
nation, and commitment to whatever goals or challenges she may
face. Marjeta always speaks with a peaceful tone. She has encouraging words to share. She is a caring and loving person. It is with
a warm and open mind that Marjeta receives her friends into her
home. Most people who have met her admire the simple manner in
which she touches their lives with her thoughtfulness. She genuinely
cares for others. Marjeta has inadvertently taught me a new dimen-
sion of love and generosity. It has been an honor and privilege for
me to join her circle of friends. Our corner of the world is a better
place because Marjeta is a part of it."*

*"I think of Marjeta as Mother Earth. She is a wonderful cook
and loves to see people enjoy her delicious and always original
food. Marjeta is a very warm, friendly, gregarious, giving, kind,
thoughtful, generous, and hospitable lady. She always has a smile
and a kind word ready."*

"A native Albanian, Marjeta Qirko speaks often and kindly of the people of her homeland and of its beautiful surroundings. A deeply religious person, she lets her early lessons in kindness, tolerance, and sharing guide her actions toward others. These principles reflect themselves in the nurturing care she provides to all she meets, be it advising students, bringing food and gifts to her colleagues and the needy in the community, and tutoring adults who have come from other countries. She is a devoted wife, mother, teacher, friend, and an excellent cook! As an immigrant herself and teacher of English as a second language at Brockton High School in Massachusetts, she can empathize with her students' challenges to succeed in a foreign land."

"Marjeta is one in a million. Brockton High School will not be the same without her. She is such a warm and caring woman. Joy just radiates from her."

"Thanks for your generous spirit, Marjeta. You are so sweet and thoughtful. You have been a blessing to many. You will be missed. Thank you for your wonderful meal today on your retirement. You have learned Mother Teresa's lessons quite well. You have brought so much happiness to so many of your students and friends. You are a saint with a heart of gold."

"What a wonderful treat! You always sure know how to share and be hospitable. There are no words to express my gratitude for everything you have done. Marjeta, what a classy gesture you made upon your retirement. You made a great difference in every life in Brockton High School. What a truly unique idea to cook and provide lunch for all of us! This was extremely generous of you. We'll miss your smiling face around here."

"It's been an honor working with you, Marjeta, all these years at Brockton High School. You'll be missed very much by everyone. Thank you so much for your kind generosity. You truly are a saint in the same way as your famous friend Mother Teresa. Thankfully for us you have left us with a wonderful legacy in Laura. Thanks to God for both of you."

"Marjeta, you have been so generous with us in your many years at Brockton High School. I know no one with a bigger and kinder heart.

Hearing your story of how you know Mother Teresa makes me think what a great humanitarian, teacher, and saint—just like you!"

Some of my mother's students wrote:

"She brings us candies and chocolates. She spends the dollars for us. That's what I want to do when I'll be a man."

"She is an excellent teacher. She is a nice person, responsible, honest, simple, smart, beautiful and respectful. I am never going to find a teacher like her. She is beautiful inside and outside. I was blessed to be her student. She is beautiful, good, and is kind to the people. I don't have anything to give to her. I have one thing to bring back to her, it's thank you so much, Mrs. Qirko."

"Mrs. Qirko is the best, excellent, and favorite teacher. She is caring and helpful. Mrs. Qirko never does wrong things for other people. Her words can help me in future. Nothing would make me happier than being your student. You have captured my heart and you will be in my heart forever. I am sure that every day in your life will be marvelous because you are such a great person."

***

My mother's generosity and blessed bread has touched all kinds of people throughout the years. One of the most heartwarming examples is how her bread touched four special children in our lives. I babysat these four children throughout my teenage years.

I babysat the children of a prominent lawyer in Brockton, Mr. Nass-ralla, whose wife, Leila, was a young woman from Lebanon. When Leila first came to America, she spoke no English; therefore, my mother was her private English teacher for one year, teaching her English through French. When she came to our house for private English lessons, she observed how mature I was for my age and told my mother that in the future when she had children, she would love it if I could be their babysitter. She kept her word.

When she had her first daughter, Louise, I was only twelve years old. She called me to be her babysitter. One year after having Louise, she had her second daughter, Rheem. Now at the age of only thirteen I was taking care of not one but two babies. I fed them, changed them, and cared for them just as if they were my own daughters. Three years later, Leila had twins, a boy named Michael and a girl named Nicole. By the age of seventeen, I was taking care of a four-year-old, a three-year-old, and two infants.

God gave me the strength and power to love and raise these children as if they were my own. My mother would bring bread with us every time we visited them. They loved my mother's blessed bread so much that they only wanted to eat my mother's bread and no other bread. They asked for it every day. The innocent smiles filled with love the minute they saw my mother take out the bread were messages that they at such young ages felt blessed by eating such bread.

Me at the age of fourteen and the first two older daughters, Louise [two years old] and Rheem [one year old].

My mother and me with the older daughter, Louise, age six, and the twins, Nicole and Michael, age two, with their mother, Leila.

Throughout the years my mother's bread has touched many lives in miraculous ways, but I am choosing to share just a few of the most miraculous stories. In 2006, after I had studied abroad in Spain, the director from the Granada Institute of International Studies, Amalia, came from Spain to visit Stonehill College. She had heard about my mother's blessed bread and was very excited when my mother invited her along with three other professors from Stonehill College to lunch at our house. Among the many ethnic dishes my mother had prepared that day, Amalia was most impressed with the bread.

On her way out, she whispered in my mother's ear: "Marjeta, could I ask you a huge favor? Can you please give me just two small slices of your bread to take with me?"

My mother immediately said, "Of course I will, with the greatest pleasure!"

My mother gave her what was left over from the bread. Amalia and the other professors left and we had no idea what she had done with that bread.

My mother with Amalia, the director of GRIIS, and two professors from Stonehill College in front of our house after the lunch.

One year later Amalia returned to Stonehill College and my mother and I visited her as she was holding a conference for the foreign language department. At the end of the conference, she said to my mother, "Marjeta, do you know what miracles your bread has done? Last year when I asked you for two slices of bread, I did not want them for myself. I wanted them for two people very dear to my heart who were facing the most difficult times in their lives. The first slice was for a very good friend of mine who was in the hospital with a terminal illness and the doctors had given her no hope. As soon as she ate your bread, within a few days the doctors were shocked to find out that everything had disappeared and she was much better. Tonight, we are having a celebration dinner with her to honor you because it was your blessing that saved her life.

"The other slice of bread was for a young woman from Guatemala who had been my housekeeper in Boston and who was engaged to a man from the Czech Republic. The two of them were suffering a lot because the woman had no documents to go to the Czech Republic and the man had no documents to come to the United States. After having eaten your blessed bread, the doors finally opened for her to complete all the documents and finally reunite with her love in the Czech Republic. Marjeta, do you see that you perform miracles because you have been blessed by the woman of miracles, Mother Teresa?"

As my mother listened to Amalia speak, her eyes filled with tears of joy. There was no greater joy for my mother than knowing she used her blessing to affect the lives of others by bringing happiness to them. It is in moments like these when my mother feels that God has blessed her with a gift to bless others and follow in the footsteps of her role model Mother Teresa.

***

The gift of Marjeta's blessed bread continues. My mother, myself, and my father visited Ronda Chervin in Connecticut in 2017. Ronda is a writer and educator, who assisted me in writing this book. She said that after eating a piece of the bread, she woke up from a nap that day with blissful joy permeating her whole body.

Ronda Chervin eating my mother's blessed bread in Connecticut.

Later, she gave a piece of it to a suffering friend of hers. This woman, Gail Arcari, inherited psoriasis from her grandmother and passed it on to her son. This began sixty years ago. She reported to Ronda: "I was blessed by the bread I ate baked by someone who knew Mother Teresa. I just ate one bite because usually gluten makes my psoriasis worse. Instead, the next day I found that it had dramatically improved, with not many red scaly patches. That lasted for several days, and then the psoriasis came back but not as bad and I haven't had any more flare ups."

Laura's Reflection on *Blessed Bread*

Witnessing the miracles and the impact that my mother's blessed bread has had on people's lives has taught me to be strong in my faith that when we believe in God and pray to Him our prayers can be answered. As my mother makes her special bread, she prays to God that whoever eats her bread may have their good wishes fulfilled. No matter what we are doing in life, it is very important to pray to God. If we pray, He will listen to our prayers and help us in whatever way He knows is best. My mother prays blessings over her bread as she makes it, fully expecting to hear about the joy that the people who eat it experience.

I want to continue this legacy by making my mother's special bread recipe and sharing it with people since Mother Teresa taught that sharing our daily bread is so important. The more we share, the more we will receive. There is no better feeling than the feeling of sharing. We should all try to share, especially food, for we will see that even small gestures will teach people the lesson of caring.

Sharing is caring and that is what we must always demonstrate to our brothers and sisters. Just as Jesus shared bread with everyone, we, too, must share our daily bread with whomever we can. If we share our daily bread, it will lead to a less hunger-stricken world. We have to always remember that bread is sacred since there are thousands and thousands of people who go hungry on a daily basis. If I teach someone to share bread and that person teaches another person who then teaches another, we will help decrease world hunger.

Study Guide Companion

- ❖ How do you define hospitality? Would you consider yourself a hospitable person? What are some practical ways to be more hospitable?

- ❖ Have you witnessed hospitality by your parents, grandparents, or other family members? How has this changed the way you view hospitality?

- ❖ How does hospitality change your perspective on human kindness?

- ❖ Do you believe hospitality is a gift from God?

- ❖ Do you usually share your food with others?
  How does this make you feel?

- ❖ When you eat lunch with colleagues, do you offer them any of the food you have, regardless if they accept it or not?

- ❖ Do you think bread is the most sacred of foods? Why or why not?

CHAPTER 28

MAKING DREAMS COME TRUE

From the time I was a little girl, I have always strived to make my dreams reality. This has not only been a goal to pursue for myself but also for others' lives. I have learned from my mother that there is joy in helping make someone's dream come true. This is worth much more than any material thing in the world. Whenever I hear what people dream of having or doing, I pin those words in my heart and never forget.

One of the best examples of making someone's dream come true

Our friend Ana in her house in Greece.

has to do with a family friend from Greece. In the summer of 2010, my family and I invited our dear friend Ana to come visit us in Boston for one month. We have known Ana our whole lives; we were neighbors in Durrës, Albania. We have some of the fondest memories of her and her parents in both their house and our house there. After we moved to the United States, Ana and her entire family moved to Greece. Though we are oceans apart, we made it a goal to see each other as much as possible throughout the years.

Upon hearing the news that we wanted her to visit, Ana could not believe her ears and was extremely happy. Coming to America was something she had always dreamed about but never thought would become reality. I was extremely happy to fulfill this dream of hers and planned to organize the trip of a lifetime for her.

As I began planning her itinerary, I remembered she had told me that one of her lifelong dreams was to see the city of Las Vegas. I called my travel agent and booked a five-day VIP trip to Las Vegas for Ana, my parents, and me. I decided to mention nothing to Ana but surprise her after she arrived in Boston. I was looking forward to seeing the excitement on her face when I told her about this side trip.

The day after she arrived in Boston, I was telling her about my recent trip to Las Vegas and that I had plenty of pictures and videos to show her to make her feel as if she were there with me. As she was watching the videos, she was delighted by the beauty of her dream city Las Vegas.

In Albanian she asked, "Laura, can I beg you for a big favor? Could you please make an extra copy of these videos for me so that when I return to Greece I can say that I had an opportunity, thanks to you, to see the magical city of Las Vegas in precise detail through your beautiful videos?"

Trying to keep a serious face, I responded, "No, Ana. I am very sorry but I can't do that for you."

She replied desperately, "Please, Laura, I beg you! This is my greatest wish!"

Again, I firmly responded, "No! I can't do that for you, but you are more than welcome to do that by yourself."

She quickly replied, "Stop playing with me! You know technology is not my strength and I have no idea of how to make a copy of the videos."

I then replied happily, "Oh, yes, I know that. That is exactly why I'm telling you that you can do your own videos tomorrow in person when we go to Las Vegas! Surprise!"

In the midst of heartfelt tears, she said, "Laura, I cannot find the words to thank you. No one has ever done something like this for me. I will never be able to thank you in this life. You are truly a blessing from above!"

Ana and me in Las Vegas in 2010.

Seeing Ana's joy made me almost explode with happiness. Something like this changes your life and helps make you become the best person you can be when you can make someone else's dreams come true.

In the summer of 2016, I was on the mission of making another dream into reality. When I was on vacation with my parents in Italy, we met the sweetest Albanian family. This family consisted of a thirty-three-year-old husband, a twenty-eight-year-old wife, a seven-year-old daughter, and a two-year-old son. This family touched our hearts because they, too, had immigrated from Albania, just like my family had immigrated from Albania to the United States.

Even though we were very similar because both our families had immigrated to a foreign land, our stories of immigration could not be more different. The young man, whose name is Arsen, had immigrated to Italy from Albania when he was a young teenager trying to escape his war-stricken country in hopes of finding a job for a better life and future in Italy. He started doing very difficult jobs in order to make money to survive in Italy. As the years progressed, he returned to Albania, got married, and brought his wife to Italy. Throughout all the difficulties and struggles they had to face as a young immigrant couple, they found the greatest joy in having children. Both of their children were born in Italy.

Arsen's family: Arsen, his wife, Roza; his daughter, Eliza; and his son, Denis, in their house in Ripa Teatina, Italy. The children are wearing clothes we sent to them from America.

What touched our hearts the most were the conditions this little family had to face daily. Arsen is the only family member who is employed. He goes to work every single day from sunrise to sunset, working at a harsh construction job, earning a very small salary in order to provide food for his family. His wife has no job because the economy in Italy is very bad, especially for immigrants. It is a hard struggle for the two of them to keep up with the house expenses and to provide food, clothes, and other necessities for their children.

When we first met them, my mother and I immediately decided to give them gifts from the United States, without even knowing them well, just to bring a little joy to their hearts. As we spent more and more time with them during our summer in Italy and became close, we decided to help them even more by giving them some money. We knew that the money we gave them was not going to save them from their financial problems, but at least they could use that money for food for a few weeks.

Knowing we were making a difference for them brought us great joy. Both husband and wife mentioned how they had always dreamed of meeting someone from America but had never thought it would come true in such an unexpected way. They had also dreamed of visiting America but believed it was impossible because of their financial problems, since traveling to America would cost them a lot of money.

My mother and father and I discussed their situation. We decided to make their dream a reality. We knew that the only family member who was an Italian citizen with an Italian passport was Arsen. His wife had come from Albania and she was not an Italian citizen; therefore, she could not travel to America. Since they loved each other so much, we knew that even if we could only make Arsen's dream of visiting America into a reality, it would be also to make both their dreams into reality. Secretly we requested information regarding Arsen's holidays, and we decided to buy him a roundtrip ticket to come to Boston.

We called him and said, "Arsen, what has been your biggest dream?"

He passionately responded, "My biggest dream is to come to America, but I know for a fact that because of my financial problems, it is an impossible dream."

I said, "What if we were to tell you that your dream is going to come true?"

He immediately replied, "No, no, it's impossible!"

"Arsen, always have faith, for it will lead you in your dream. We have turned your dream into a reality by buying you a roundtrip ticket with all costs included to come as our guest to our home in Brockton."

Upon hearing this news, Arsen, his wife, and the children were all in major shock.

Arsen said, "Marjeta, Laura, and Fredi, I don't have any words to thank you. I cannot express the gratitude I feel for what you are doing. I cannot describe the happiness I am feeling at this moment. Something like this no one in my entire life has ever done, not even my parents. I am most thankful to God who sent me the most special, blessed people."

After we returned from Italy to Boston, we counted down each month until his trip by sending monthly packages filled with presents and money for all the members of the family. The excitement we felt when they received these gifts as they counted down each month to his arrival in Boston was such a beautiful feeling. What a priceless joy to see pictures of the children wearing the clothes we bought for them, playing with the toys we sent, and thanking us with smiles filled with joy and love. Making dreams come true for others makes our dreams come true.

Arsen arrived in Boston on April 13, 2017, and spent ten of what he described as some of the most memorable days of his life. They will be imprinted on his mind and heart forever. Since the first day Arsen arrived in Boston, my family made sure that he experienced the trip of a lifetime. We dedicated our time to taking him to the best locations, tourist attractions, and restaurants. We wanted to give him the royal treatment filled with love. We wanted him to feel as if he was home, even though he was thousands of miles away. Upon his departure, I asked Arsen to give me his impressions of his trip to Boston, Massachusetts, visiting the Qirko family.

Arsen, his eyes filled with tears of joy, said, "Throughout my entire life, I had always dreamed of visiting the country of my dreams, America, but I never imagined how this impossible dream could become reality. Thanks to all of you, you made my dream a reality. What I have experienced in America these past ten days have not felt like the fairy tale I had imagined before my trip but ten times better, exceeding all my expectations. I never thought I would visit and see so many places in such a short amount of time and experience so many gestures of love from all of you along the way.

"You not only hosted me in your home, but you accompanied me every single day to different beautiful cities and tourist attractions. You opened my eyes and made me see things that I had only seen in movies or in dreams. You brought me to fancier restaurants than I had ever imagined and treated me with high-quality food from breakfast to lunch to dinner that went beyond my expectations. You not only paid my ticket to come to America, but you did not let me spend even one penny from my pocket during the entire duration of my stay.

"Now I am a true believer that good people in this world with genuine hearts do exist because you are living proof. You not only thought of my happiness but also the happiness of all my family members. You prepared three suitcases filled with presents and goodies for my entire family, including my wife and children, my parents, my siblings, my wife's parents, and my wife's siblings, as well as many other children in Ripa Teatina, Italy.

"On top of everything, you gave me money for my family, for my parents, and for my wife's parents. This is a noble gesture that leaves me speechless because there is no one else in the world today who would make such gestures of love, expecting nothing in return. I have never known people who put others' dreams in front of their own. You are the only people I know who feel that your dreams are becoming reality by making others' dreams come true. Forever I will be thankful for you! These ten days in America with such a special family were memorable days that will be imprinted on my mind and heart forever. You have become and will always be the dearest people in my heart."

Hearing this from Arsen brought us great joy. Witnessing Arsen's dream become reality made our dream of helping people come true in a very special way.

Laura's Reflection on *Making Dreams Come True*

When we make others' dreams come true, our dreams will also often come true. Just as I have been a believer that the more you give, the more you will receive, I have also become a true dreamer that if you help make someone's dream become a reality, your dreams will often come to pass.

I recall that in the spring of 2016, I was in the process of making someone else's dream come true. Without expecting anything in return, all my time, all my dedication, all my love was put into make this person's dream of pursuing a career in the United States come true. One year later, in the spring of 2017, I found myself in what seemed like a dream since other people were now working to make my dream of publishing Humanitarian Woman come true.

Just like I helped someone else make their dream a reality, God was repaying me by sending other people to help make my dream come true. Have you ever found yourself in the situation that after having helped someone, you were also helped? This is how God repays every good deed. There is no better feeling in this world than the feeling of bringing joy to others and fulfilling their greatest wishes.

Study Guide Companion

❖ What has been your greatest dream in life?

❖ Have you ever helped fulfill someone else's dream? How has that made you feel?

❖ Do you believe that when you help make others' dreams a reality, your own dreams will become reality as well?

CHAPTER 29

DESTINY CONNECTS PEOPLE

All my life, especially after having been blessed by Mother Teresa, I have believed some people come in our lives as blessings. I am a true believer that God brings the right people into our lives at the right moments. God often welcomes people into our lives when we least expect it. Destiny always finds a way to connect good people with one another.

In December 2015, I visited someone very dear to my heart in Italy to spend the holiday season together. My last night in Italy was extremely bittersweet for me, knowing I had to leave this person and all the beautiful moments we shared during my stay there. As I spent a sleepless night counting the minutes, I sent a message to my mother in the United States, telling her how heartbroken I felt to leave Italy.

My mother, trying to cheer me up, said, "Laura, I have a feeling your trip tomorrow will be great because a person you will meet on the plane is destined to be in your life."

Because I have traveled on planes hundreds of times and sat next to many different people, I could have had faith in my mother's words. But it was just so difficult for me at that moment in my life.

My mother's words came true in the most unexpected way. The next morning my first flight took two hours from Bologna, Italy, to Munich, Germany. My second flight was a nine-hour flight from Munich, Germany, to Boston, Massachusetts. Due to a weather delay, my flight from Italy arrived in Germany only twenty minutes before my second flight for Boston left. When I landed in Germany, all I could think about was how I was going to catch my next plane. I had promised to call my friend in Italy as soon as I landed in Munich, Germany; however, there was no time.

I had a dilemma. I could either use the time to make a phone call or I could catch the flight for Boston. Overwhelmed with panic, I entered the plane out of breath, and I sat down next to a lovely lady. Right away she noticed that I was extremely sad and said, "Honey, you made it, take a seat and relax; everything will be okay. You made it to the plane on time."

I looked at her and said, "Thank you, miss, it's been such a rough day for me having to leave Italy and someone dear to my heart. What's worse is that since my flight from Bologna, Italy, arrived twenty minutes ago, I could not keep a promise. I had promised my dear friend in Italy to call as soon as I arrived in Munich, Germany, but I had no way of doing that if I wanted to be on this flight."

As she saw the desperation in my eyes, she said, "Here you go, please use my phone to send a message, notifying your friend you are okay."

I accepted her offer with a big smile on my face. After I got through to my friend in Italy, she asked, "Where are you from?"

"My name is Laura Qirko. I am from Brockton, Massachusetts. I'm a foreign language teacher at Brockton High School and I was on vacation in Italy for my Christmas break."

She replied, "My name is Anne. I am also from Boston. I work in Charleston for Massachusetts Eye and Ear Hospital."

Upon finding out that Anne was from the same area I was, I felt more at ease. During our conversation, we discovered we had a lot of things in common. I told her about my personal reason for taking the trip to Italy, and she was touched by my beautiful story. She was happy to see me go from being so sad and heartbroken about my past, to being happy and optimistic about the future.

We entered into a deep conversation for the entire nine hours' duration of the flight. The nine-hour flight seemed like it took only one hour. Even though we had just met, I felt spiritually connected to this wonderful woman as if she was my personal support sent from God at the moment I needed her most. My mother's words kept ringing in my ears. She had reassured me the previous night that I would meet someone on the plane who would change my frame of mind. When we arrived in Boston, the woman and I exchanged phone numbers and promised each other we would keep in touch.

I kept my promise and within a week of returning home, I decided to call her. The moment Anne heard my voice, she said, "Laura, I am so happy you called me. I have been thinking of you this whole week because you were an angel sent from above for me. Laura, you have no idea how much you helped me that day on the plane. You have no idea what I was going through!

"That day on the plane, I was going through the difficult pain of losing someone very dear to my heart while I was on vacation in Italy. My entire vacation was crushed by the tragedy, causing me to have the worst days of my life. That day flying back home was a day I had been dreading ever since I found out the tragic news; however, you were a ray of sunshine who brightened my mood. It was as if God sent you there because it was destined for us to meet. As a matter of fact, my husband and I changed seats on the plane at the last minute, and I truly believe it was destiny that arranged this change in order to bring us together."

With tears in my eyes, I said, "Anne, I wanted to thank you because you were like a guardian angel sent from God to help me through my so very difficult time. Destiny brought us together and I believe that it is destiny that we become the best of friends. That day you played the role of a best friend, sister, aunt, mother—someone I looked up to for guidance and support. Destiny always finds a way to bring good people together and that day was truly a blessing for us both."

Anne and me at my brother's wedding.

Since that day on the plane, Anne has been there for me through some of the most difficult and some of the happiest times of my life, dedicating time and love to me and my entire family. She has helped me in the healing process through some very difficult situations. She has brought love and joy to my heart throughout our happiest occasions. In such a short time we have become inseparable friends and I am sure we were always destined to be blessings for each other.

As Mother Teresa taught us: always have faith, for it is faith that will guide our destiny.

Laura's Reflection on *Destiny Connects People*

Meeting Anne, a stranger who has become very dear to me, has taught me to always believe in destiny, especially when it comes to meeting people who will be special in my life. By destiny, I mean things coming together in life unexpectedly. Even if a person enters your life who is wrong for you, God will make sure that the person eventually exits your life. Have you ever thought how lucky you have been to welcome a very special person into your life or to have someone who is bad for you exit your life?

I believe this has to do with destiny. Destiny is what happens in our lives outside of our control, but it is part of our path in life. God guides us. Destiny connects people all over the world. If we believe in God, all things are possible.

In Albanian, we have a saying: "Destiny is written, and if things are destined to be, they will be."

Study Guide Companion

❖ Do you believe there is a destiny for your life?

❖ Have you ever met a special person or people who seemed to cross your path out of nowhere?

❖ How do you define divine providence?

❖ Has God ever connected you with an extra-special person?

❖ Do you believe things happen in life by accident or coincidence?

❖ Do you believe there are things in your life that are meant to be?

CHAPTER 30

A HUMANITARIAN AT HEART

My mother follows in the footsteps of Mother Teresa each time she returns to our beloved country, Albania. When my mother plans a trip to our home country, she becomes extremely excited. This is not because she is going on vacation and will have a good time but because she will have the opportunity to buy and give everyone presents to make them happy.

After deciding she will go to Albania, my mother goes shopping every day, buying presents for her relatives, dear friends, and even people she does not yet know whom she anticipates meeting. My mother usually goes to Albania to collect her pension, since she worked as an English teacher there for more than twenty-three years. Even though her pension is very low, she collects it throughout the year in order to do good deeds with it, especially for the elderly.

When we originally left Albania to come to the United States, one of the most difficult parts was leaving behind our dear friends. As the years have passed, friends of ours who are in Albania have still remained friends always in our hearts. Even though we have been separated for years, my mother still keeps all the memories quite vivid. She never forgets them and they are the first people she thinks of when she receives her pension money.

As soon as my mother is given her pension money in Albania, she calls all her old friends and tells them to also invite other friends of theirs and gathers them for a fancy lunch or dinner in a beautiful restaurant. After she treats them all to lunch or dinner, she takes them shopping and asks them to choose whatever they want my mother to buy them. She also brings small gifts and gives each of them a little money to buy what they please. My mother knows that what she is giving to them will not solve any problems they might have or make them rich; however, what will make them rich is the happiness my mother will bring them by making such a gesture.

My mother with her Albanian friends, treating them to lunch in 2014 and 2015.

My mother does such things, not only with dear friends of ours but also with people she does not even know. In Albania, I recall a time we were with my mother in an elevator. My mother noticed an old man whom she did not know and took out a ten-dollar bill from her pocketbook and gave it to him saying: "Sir, please take this money and enjoy a coffee with your friends." The value of the money did not affect the man at all; however, the gesture is something that I'm certain will be imprinted on his mind forever.

Besides such gifts, she also often sends her friends money via Western Union and packages on a weekly basis. My mother might be the most famous and well-known name at Western Union because she regularly sends money all around the world. She is also a well-known person at the post office as she sends packages to people all around the world on a weekly basis. Many people ask my mother, "Why do you do this?"

Her simple answer is, "Because I am privileged to follow in the footsteps of the most humanitarian woman on earth, Mother Teresa!"

***

Marika, the woman from Greece, with a happy face after my mother took her and her husband food shopping.

An example from another country was when my mother traveled to Greece for a few weeks after she had visited Albania. She wanted to visit with dear elderly family friends of ours. My mother felt great joy the day she took the elderly couple to a supermarket and said, "Please choose whatever you desire and fill up the cart for a months' worth of food, and it will be my greatest pleasure to pay." This gesture impressed that couple so much because not even their own children or grandchildren had ever thought of offering them such a gift. They looked at my mother as their angel not because my mother saved them from financial problems, but because someone recognized they truly have worth.

***

My mother leaves her humanitarian legacy wherever in the world she sets foot. During a vacation in Paris, we were in a Metro station and my mother saw a crippled woman lying on the floor with a sign that said, "Pour mes enfants!," which in English means "for my children." My mother automatically reached in her pocket and gave the woman a twenty-dollar bill, which fifteen years ago was worth a lot. The woman was so overtaken by my mother's generous gesture that she followed my mother with her eyes until the train left the station. My mother did not know this woman nor will she ever see her again; however, the satisfaction was so great knowing she had made a small difference in the woman's life even for that one day.

At that moment my mother thought of one of Mother Teresa's famous quotes: "At the end of life we will not be judged by how many diplomas we have received, how much money we have made, how many great things we have done. We will be judged by 'I was hungry, and you gave me something to eat, I was naked and you clothed me. I was homeless, and you took me in.'"

***

That same year in Paris, we stayed at a very beautiful hotel in the center of the city where all the housekeeping staff were immigrants from Francophone-African countries. My mother felt bad seeing them work so hard every day. Her heart broke when she discovered that they made very little money for all the hard work and dedication they put into their jobs. She decided to do something to bring them a little happiness and brighten their days. My mother called all the maids of the hotel and decided to give them different gifts and some money since she felt bad that they were immigrants struggling to make a living. She remembered when she first immigrated to the United States that any help someone offered made a big difference in your life.

***

Another similar situation happened in London. We were on a guided tour near Saint Paul's Cathedral and my father went to use the restroom. Upon returning, he told my mother that there was a poor immigrant woman who was cleaning the bathrooms. My mother went to where the woman was, took off her necklace, and gave it to her saying, "Take this! It is a present for you!"

The woman could not believe her eyes. She kept saying, "Madame, is this for me? No! It's impossible; I don't believe it! No one has ever done something like this for me."

My mother gave her a hug and said, "I hope what I gave you will bring you blessings!"

The happiness my mother felt in giving this stranger her necklace is something that is worth more than any material thing in the world.

***

My mother is not only a humanitarian with people but also with nations. She is especially concerned for African and Haitian communities. When my mother worked at Brockton High School, there was a French teacher who had come as an exchange teacher from Senegal. My mother felt bad for her, knowing she had several young children to support in the United States. My mother would prepare and bring her lunch on a daily basis. Throughout the three years this woman taught there, my mother and I would go shopping every weekend and buy clothes and toys and bring them to her to hopefully take to Senegal when she returned home.

After two years had passed, my mother went to bring her lunch and could not find her. When the teacher came back to school, my mother asked where she had been the day she was absent. She explained that she had been in New York City where she had sent a huge container by ship to Senegal with all the presents my mother had given her for the Senegalese people.

My mother's eyes filled with tears of joy upon hearing this news because she knew she would make the poorest people happy when they received these presents. They would think these were presents sent from God.

Each year my mother and I also donate clothes, house accessories, and money to the poor people of Haiti, which is the poorest country in the western hemisphere. Because my mother and I have taught students from Haiti, especially those affected by the horrific earthquake, we have made it our goal to donate as much as we can every single year. There is no happier feeling for us than knowing we are putting a smile on people's faces and brightening their lives.

As Mother Teresa said, a smile is the greatest symbol of love. If we bring love to one person and that one person brings love to another, we can live in a much more peaceful world.

Laura's Reflection on *A Humanitarian at Heart*

Witnessing my mother be a humanitarian at heart taught me to be the best humanitarian I can be, just like her. My mother decided to become an even greater humanitarian after her special meeting with Mother Teresa as a way to set an example for me to become one too. Together, we are hoping to encourage everyone in the world to be humanitarians and philanthropists whenever they can. People should always try to give to others no matter how little. The quantity does not matter; it's the quality of the gesture that matters.

Everyone in the world should be charitable givers, whether by donating food, clothes, supplies, or love to the people of their own communities or to those far from home. It is good to be sharing with people of different backgrounds, for example, being sure to smile at a cashier in the supermarket, especially if he or she is not of your nationality.

By helping people in whatever way possible, we will be changing them to become happier people filled with love. We need to promote human welfare. We must try to always be philanthropists. Our goal should be to find ways to improve the lives of all our brothers and sisters in the world. When people in the world are happy, we will live in a much more peaceful universe.

Study Guide Companion

❖ What is your definition of being a humanitarian?

❖ Do you know a humanitarian person? How does witnessing what this person does change your life?

❖ Would you consider yourself to be a humanitarian?

CHAPTER 31

BLESSED DATES

Many people may think that dates mean nothing, but I truly believe that dates hold a powerful message. In my family, we have experienced dates as powerful factors in regard to our connection with Mother Teresa.

My mother and I have had such a strong spiritual connection with Mother Teresa since the day she blessed us. My brother has also had a very unique connection with Mother Teresa. Our entire journey with Mother Teresa began the day my mother received the unexpected knock at the door with the news that she was wanted to teach the Sisters of Mother Teresa on September 23. That day of the year, September 23, is my brother's birthday. It was on his birthday when our experience began.

Even though my brother had such a strong connection to Mother Teresa since he had the privilege of being baptized in the presence of the Sisters of Mother Teresa, we never imagined that one day in the future my brother and Mother Teresa would share another one of the important dates of their lives.

The year 2016 was a big year for my brother because that was when he was going to get married. The year 2016 also was one of most important years for the world because that was the year that the Catholic Church in Rome officially recognized Mother Teresa as a saint. The canonization of Mother Teresa was set for September 4, 2016. For my family, this was going to be a most blessed date, since we had all been personally blessed by Mother Teresa. However, my brother could never have imagined that the day Mother Teresa was recognized as a saint would be the same day he would become a husband.

My brother's wedding did take place the same day as the canonization of Mother Teresa: September 4, 2016.

Now, see how graces of prayer were interwoven in this event.

In November 2015, my brother became engaged. The couple decided they wanted to get married in September 2016. At the beginning of 2016, we started looking at venues for the wedding. There was one dream venue that my brother and the entire family wanted: Ocean Cliff in Newport, Rhode Island.

Because people plan weddings a year or two years in advance, we feared it was going to be difficult for us to find an open date for September 2016. To make matters even more complicated, my mother was praying to have the wedding on September 4, 2016, the date for Mother Teresa's canonization. Eager to make her dream into reality, my mother called Ocean Cliff to set up an appointment for the wedding, mentioning that the couple requested a September day.

My mother was told that, unfortunately, everything was already booked for September 2016. At this moment, hoping for a miracle, my mother said the prayer Mother Teresa taught her. Then she asked the woman to double check one more time. The prayer of Mother Teresa must have gone directly to God's ears because the woman on the phone replied, "Mrs. Qirko, we only have one opening, which is Sunday, September 4, 2016!"

My mother, quickly replied, "We will be more than honored to take it!"

I believe this was a miracle from above because this is the date my mother had always dreamed of but never thought could happen.

Mother Teresa's presence radiated throughout my brother's entire wedding. One week before the wedding, the news stations were discussing the powerful and dangerous hurricane that was going to strike New England on Sunday, September 4. Up until the Saturday before the wedding, my mother was praying for a miracle to change the weather because the wedding ceremony was going to be held outside, overlooking the sea.

Until the day before the wedding, weathermen were warning people to take shelter from the hurricane. Upon hearing this devastating news, all of us were worried that the hurricane was going to ruin my brother's wedding day. However, God knew this was going to be a most blessed day for my brother.

Thanks to Mother Teresa's blessing and the spiritual connection she has with my mother, September 4, 2016, surprisingly turned out to be a gorgeous, perfect, sunny day set for a fairy-tale wedding. We could have not asked for a more beautiful wedding from start to finish.

I believe it was God's blessing that postponed the hurricane that was predicted to strike Sunday until Monday, the day after the wedding. God knew that the same day the Catholic Church recognized Mother Teresa as a saint would also be the most precious day for my brother as well, since God had personally blessed him years before by the laying on of hands by Mother Teresa.

My brother, Dritan, and his wife, Alkina, on their wedding day.

My family at my brother's wedding on September 4, 2016.

***

Mother Teresa and I also share a very special date, October 19. In Albania, October 19 is a national holiday—Mother Teresa's Day! October 19, 2016, was even more wonderful because there was a beautiful celebration of Mother Teresa's sainthood.

For me October 19 is a special day because it is my saint's name day: Saint Laura's Day. Saint Laura was born in Cordoba, Spain. She became a nun at Cuteclara after losing her husband. She was tragically scalded to death by her Moorish captors. I truly believe that Saint Teresa of Calcutta and Saint Laura of Cordoba have a spiritual connection, the same connection Mother Teresa had with a little girl named Laura. We are destined to be spiritually connected for life through this blessed date.

Four plus nineteen make twenty-three, the three blessed dates that were destined for my family and me!

September 4, October 19, September 23

Laura's Reflection on *Blessed Dates*

Having so many blessed dates that I cherish in my heart has taught me that dates really do hold special meanings. We must pay close attention to all the important dates in our lives; when we do, we can find unusual connections. Before finding out that in Albania October 19 was declared Mother Teresa Day, I had no idea how much more special my saint day was. We all have important dates in our lives—our birthdays, name days, wedding days, and so forth. If we examine each date, we might find it has a connection with other important dates in our lives.

Study Guide Companion

❖ Are there dates in your life that are important to you?

❖ Can you write down three or four dates and explain why they are important to you?

❖ Have you ever made a spiritual connection with any of your important dates?

CHAPTER 32

THE BOND OF A LIFETIME

Since the day Mother Teresa chose me out of everyone in the crowd and gave me the silver medallion until the day she personally blessed me, God has formed a real spiritual bond between us. That same bond formed in my heart as a child remains with me today in the spirit of Mother Teresa. The bond with Mother Teresa will be a lifetime bond because I will always strive to follow in her footsteps.

I will devote myself to spreading Christ's message of forgiving others in the spirit of Mother Teresa. Like her I will share my daily bread with any needy person I meet. I will follow her message of unconditional love. Mother Teresa exhorts people around the world to be missionaries of love. In Mother Teresa's eyes a person is God's love in action. Through each of us, God is loving the world every day.

My mother and I have always hoped that when people come into contact with us, they will become different and better people because of having met us. We must always radiate God's love every opportunity we get. We must take advantage of the present and not dwell on the past. We must take advantage today, and not wait for tomorrow.

By constantly achieving these missions throughout life, I will be blessed with a bond of a lifetime as a Humanitarian Woman.

Laura's Reflection on *The Bond of a Lifetime*

As a child, forming the cherished bond with Mother Teresa taught me that some bonds last a lifetime. Many times we find that one person or a family are bonded to us. We need to cherish those bonds in our hearts. Just as I have let the bond with Mother Teresa lead me to do humanitarian acts, we should honor those bonds because they are eternal.

Study Guide Companion

❖ Have you formed a close bond with someone in your life? How has this bond affected your life?

❖ Do you believe that some bonds are never meant to be broken?

❖ Do you have a lifetime bond with someone? Why and how is that person special for you?

LAURA'S FINAL REFLECTION

As I bring my book to a conclusion, I just want to say how privileged I am to have shared a big part of my life with you.

You, my dear reader, might wonder after reading Touched by a Saint that by having such an incredibly busy life working on so many different projects, when do I ever have time for myself or to go out with friends or even develop personal relationships?

People who volunteered to read earlier versions of this manuscript approached me with some questions of a very personal nature that were not addressed in the manuscript. These questions made me think that it would be important for me to give you, my new friend, one final reflection.

Throughout my hectic schedule, the one thing I surely always make time for is meeting new people and forming new friendships and personal relationships. Being a young woman with a passion for traveling the world gives me the opportunity to meet and network with new people often. During the past fifteen years, I have been blessed with some beautiful friendships that I cherish to this day.

I want to let you in on a little secret about myself. If you haven't figured it out yet, I am a bit of an old soul that came from old-school Europe. I am one of those who still believe in God's divine providence, that God has a plan for my life that includes that special somebody for my future.

For now, I will continue working in my passion and calling as a humanitarian woman, never forgetting how my personal encounters with Mother Teresa changed my life forever.

DEDICATED TO THE MEMORY OF
MOTHER TERESA